WITHNAIL AND I

WITHNAIL AND I

BRUCE ROBINSON

BLOOMSBURY

First published in Great Britain 1989

Movie copyright © 1986 Paragon Entertainment Corporation

Screenplay copyright © 1989 by Bruce Robinson

New Introduction © 1995 by Bruce Robinson

This paperback edition published 1995

The moral right of the author has been asserted

Bloomsbury Publishing Plc, 2 Soho Square, London W1V 6HB

A CIP catalogue record for this book
is available from the British Library

10 9 8 7 6 5 4 3 2

ISBN 0 7475 2358 4

Typeset by Hewer Text Composition Services, Edinburgh
Printed in Great Britain by St Edmundsbury Press, Suffolk

For Viv

INTRODUCTION

This is almost certainly the last time I'll ever write anything about *Withnail and I*. Just in case it doesn't come out too good I'll get to the point immediately. I want to dedicate this new edition to my friend Vivian. Under normal circumstances (and in respect of Viv) I'd have put some effort into this, worried about it for a week, and spent another writing it. But I'm feeling un-normal. I've got two different headaches. One on top of the brain the size of a fried egg. And the other about a yard long hanging off my left eye. You don't want the details, but I went on holiday and an Italian gave me a poisoned oyster. This is the only true thing I'm going to tell you here. So far this bastard snail has cost me over two thousand pounds in the Nuffield Hospital, and busted every deadline I promised Bloomsbury. I promised a fax in about an hour but I won't be sending it because I haven't written it. And I can tell you I'm panicking. I just phoned them up and told them the fax machine was down, but that I had a repair man on the way who arrived and assured me transmission would be available by twelve o'clock. Now it's two-forty-five, and I'm considering phoning them back and telling them the fax repair man just died. 'I'm sorry about this, but I've got a body in the room, I'll have to post the introduction tomorrow.' But they're not going to believe me. After all the bullshit I've pumped out over the last three weeks, they're not going to believe anything. What they absolutely one hundred per cent *know*, is that I haven't written it yet. What they don't know, is that I *can't*. I'm on two pints of intravenous antibiotic a day, and it's given me the block. I simply can't find the wherewithal for the words I want. So what I'm going to have to do is commit the unthinkable and steal some old ones.

From 1966 to about 1976, I kept a diary, and page after page of this is about Vivian and I. I met him in 1964 in our first year in drama school. He wore a blue suit and shades and looked like Marlon Brando. Everyone thought he was going to be a star. Within ten minutes I was his closest friend, and so was everyone else. Everyone loved Viv. He wasn't a bad actor (though when we left Central School he hardly ever got a job). Wasn't a bad writer either (although I don't ever remember him writing anything). The reality is that, if he had acted, or had written, he wouldn't have excelled at either because the interest wasn't there. What Vivian was brilliant at was being Vivian. That was his genius, and everyone who ever met him was overwhelmed by it. His nicknames were 'the spine' and 'crime'. I don't know where the first came from, but the latter predicated on his ability to spend all day in the pub, and always with discretion navigate his turn to buy a drink. 'Crime doesn't pay.' But none of us cared because his company was worth the price. Viv was into literature, Keats and Beaudelaire, and turned me on to both these poets. Plus the funniest book I've ever read, the great À *Rebours*, is one of two novels Marwood shoves into his suitcase at the end of the film.

There isn't a line of Viv's in *Withnail and I*, but his

horrible wine-stained tongue may as well have spoken every word. Without Viv, this story could never have been written. And all I've got to do is look back through this old diary with its daisies stuck under yellowing Sellotape, to realise why. Vivian and I lived *Withnail and I* for a long time before that weird thing happened in my head, and I had to sit at the kitchen table and try and write it down.

April 16 1975
Hadn't seen V. for two years. He's lost his looks but not his habit. Scotch before breakfast. He doesn't eat breakfast. Vivian is drinking himself to death. He said, 'If there's a God, why are arses at the perfect height for kicking?' and I said 'I've got to agree with you.'

Going backwards now and plunging deep into the hangovers. I can't believe the amount of hangovers.

November 16 1969
In bed for two days. I can hear Viv groaning in the other room. I can't believe this one. It's almost biblical.

I simply can't believe the amount of drinking. Practically every entry starts with a description of a hangover, and they are all different, like Eskimos have twenty different ways of describing snow. This one was gin and retsina and lasted four and a half days. It gets about a page and a half, adjectives all over it, as I looked for different ways to describe pain. In the middle of it there was a knock on the door, that kind of banging that means that someone wants money. It went away and came back at ten. I needed somebody else's God to get out of the fucking bed. Viv was already in the hall wearing somebody else's mac. 'What do you want?' he said. 'I've come to cut you off,' said the cunt, 'I'm North Thames Gas.' He got up a ladder he'd brought with him, and said, 'Which is your meter?' 'That one,' I said, too ill to be dishonest. 'No it isn't,' said Vivian, 'it's the other one.' And the representative of the board went about the business of cutting off the gas to the flat downstairs. An hour later we broke into it and stole his Scotch. Vivian was of the opinion that the only way to deal with a hangover was to drink your way around it. Jesus, I remember you drinking them out. I remember you drinking the lighter fuel in the middle of a blistering argument. But I'd forgotten that I was a member of the Conservative Party.

January 16 1970

V. came back and said we should join the Conservative Party. 'What for?' I said. 'Because they give you sherry.' (Apparently he'd met some accountant called Bill Twococks who told him this was the case.) That night we got on our suits and walked over to Primrose Hill. The Conservative Party was in a basement and consisted of about six women and a photo of MacMillan on the wall. A tall twot with a ludicrous accent and a second-hand Saab wanted us to 'canvass'. We said we would, but didn't get any sherry, so we threw their fucking leaflets over a hedge.

April 30 1969

Vivian and I get on our suits and go down for wine-tasting at Sotheby's. This time we didn't get in. Some bloke with ears and a green hat prevented our entry. 'We've come to taste the wine,' we said. 'You two cunts can hop it,' he said. He obviously remembered us from previous tastings and this explusion left us depressed. Sotheby's was one of the best shows in town to drink brilliant wine and arsehole yourself absolutely free.

That night we go into Regent's Park and look at the wolves. I can't count the number of times we went into the park and looked at the wolves. And I can't believe Vivian is dead. He got cancer of the throat and they tore his voice out. And the fellow I'd always thought of as being the biggest coward I'd ever met materialised into the bravest bastard I'd ever known. It's got to be hard to laugh when you're dying, but I'll always remember you laughing. That sad, brilliant, bitter face of yours laughing. Goodbye my darling friend. This is for you for ever. And I know if there's a pub in heaven, you'll be in it. And Keats will be buying the drinks.

B.R. August 1995

CAST LIST

WITHNAIL	RICHARD E. GRANT
. . . AND I	PAUL MCGANN
MONTY	RICHARD GRIFFITHS
DANNY	RALPH BROWN
JAKE	MICHAEL ELPHICK
IRISHMAN	DARAGH O'MALLEY
ISACS PARKIN	MICHAEL WARDLE
MRS PARKIN	UNA BRANDON-JONES
GENERAL	NOEL JOHNSON
WAITRESS	IRENE SUTCLIFFE
TEA SHOP PROPRIETOR	LLEWELLYN REES
POLICEMAN ONE	ROBERT OATES
POLICEMAN TWO	ANTHONY WISE
PRESUMING ED	EDDIE TAGOE

A HANDMADE FILMS PRODUCTION
MUSIC BY DAVID DUNDAS AND RICK WENTWORTH
CO-PRODUCED BY DAVID WIMBURY
EXECUTIVE PRODUCERS GEORGE HARRISON AND
    DENIS O'BRIEN
PRODUCED BY PAUL HELLIER
WRITTEN AND DIRECTED BY BRUCE ROBINSON

· WITHNAIL AND I

1. INT. APARTMENT. DAY.
Low-quality daylight . . . dawn light . . . here comes some
music . . . King Curtis on sax . . . a magnificent rendition
of 'A Whiter Shade of Pale' . . . so sweet . . . so sour . . .
this is beautiful.

WITHNAIL AND I

In big letters as the solo begins. Principal titles will
continue over this room. Despite the squalor the room is
furnished with antiques . . . heirlooms and other quality
stuff . . . an indescribable mélange *of stuff crowds a low*
table. A large Victorian globe of the world soars above
bacon rinds. Objets d'art *and breakfast remains compete*
for space.

Dostoyevsky described hell as perhaps nothing more
than a room with a chair in it. This room has several
chairs. A young man sits in one. He isn't comfortable. He
is leaning forward. He is scrutinising his thumbs. He is
wired. Now he's lighting a cigarette. Now nothing is
moving but cigarette smoke. And no sound other than the
beautiful lachrymose saxophone.

The man in the chair is MARWOOD. *Twenty-five years*
old. Milk white with insomnia. Glasses like Lennon's and
a sweet face behind them. Seventy-five per cent good looks

1

and the rest is anxiety. This is a long haul with unspecified destination. Only thing certain is there are still hours to go. Hours and hours have stagnated in here. Drifting in cigarette smoke and settling with the dust.

And everything looks ill. The walls and furniture look ill. Daylight looks ill. He exhales a huge bouquet of smoke. It's blue. Shifts again and runs hands through his hair. It's black and could do with a dose of Vosene.

MARWOOD *reaches for a bottle of beer instead. Swallows a stale inch with eyes on the move . . . they navigate the globe and it seems to disgust him. Keep moving and good God in heaven is* this *what he* sees?

2. P.O.V. MARWOOD.
A kitchen extends off the living room. But much worse. The living room doesn't have a sink. This room does and it looks like it's vomited. The unwashed and the unwashable are stacked to the height of the taps. Every horizontal surface is covered in naso-visual horror. Here are the remains of fish suppers and the newspapers in which they were dispensed. Here are saucepans filled with unspeakable liquids. Here are empty wine bottles and dead flowers. Roses in black water like knuckles of congealed blood. Here is a frying pan driven vertically *with a partially fried egg still attached . . .*

3. INT. KITCHEN. APARTMENT. DAY.
The view stops MARWOOD *in his tracks. He's come in here and brought the titles with him. He stares, as though witnessing this panorama of degradation for the first time.*

Something must be done to maintain equilibrium. His

2

eyes settle on a kettle. A decision is taken. Plunging at the sink he fills it with water and slams his kettle on the gas.

A hypnotic blue flame circles the kettle. For a moment it demands his attention. But this thing's beginning to freak him out . . . the flame is devouring all the oxygen supplies . . . like the whole fucking house is having an asthma attack.

No air in here and he heads back to the living room. But the camera doesn't bother to follow (it's seen this journey a hundred times before). It stays here with the kettle and flame and lets him pace in the distance of the apartment.

There he goes past the globe. And here he is coming back again. Now he's looking in the mirror. Now re-observing his thumbs. Looks like he's taking his pulse (but maybe that's an illusion). Now suddenly another decision is made and he stubs his cigarette . . . scarf on . . . long black overcoat on . . . some kind of limit seems to have been reached. Now he's on his way through the kitchen door and the music and camera must follow.

4. INT. STAIRWAY. APARTMENT. DAY.
Too dark to see anything much out here. Boots clatter on carpetless stairs. MARWOOD *reaches the bottom and knocks on a door.*

MARWOOD: I'm going for a cup of tea . . . (*Silence.*)
D'you want one? (*Silence.*) D'you want a cup of tea, Withnail?

WITHNAIL (*O.S.*): No.

MARWOOD *is already on the move. Motoring on bile he descends more stairs. Hits a front door and slams the music behind him.*

3

5. EXT. STREET. CAMDEN TOWN. DAWN.
A boarded-up warehouse opposite. A clapped-out Jaguar parked outside a line of old dwellings. MARWOOD *emerges from one of them. Fills his lungs before heading up the street.*

MARWOOD (*V.O. – playback*): . . . perhaps thirteen million people in London. And if they all go once a day, that means end to end there'd be enough shit to stretch from here to Casablanca . . .

6. EXT. ALLEYWAY. CAMDEN TOWN. DAWN.
The street lights are still on. Utterly dismal. A carbon copy of a day. MARWOOD *scurries and the camera hurries with him. Their combined speed puts the dripping alley in a blur.*

MARWOOD (*V.O.*): I'm not working it out now. I'd done that before with Withnail. Also computed the Dresden route via Cologne. And Moscow in a day and a half . . .
Still hanging in as close as it can the camera turns a corner and now they're under a railway bridge. Rain hangs like dirty tinsel. The area is as shabby as the weather.

MARWOOD (*V.O.*): Thirteen million people in London, and Withnail's gotta be the only one who would bother to work that out. Why would he work that out? The bastard must be unique.
An old HEAP *under the bridge is selling newspapers. His face glows in the light of a carbide lamp. A billboard announces that a 'Vicar Batters Old Woman to Death in Sex Outrage'. Before* MARWOOD *realises it he has stopped to buy a newspaper.*

4

MARWOOD: *Evening News* please.

A good middle-class accent. Blank response from the
HEAP.

Evening News please.

OLD HEAP: It's Sunday morning, mate . . .

7. INT. WANKER'S CAFÉ. CAMDEN TOWN. DAY.

A dozen eggs billow in a massive pan. This is full-
frontal frying and you can hear them flap. A spatula
goes in and a pair are hauled out and slid on to a
plate. Big close up it crosses the café revealing
MARWOOD *as it passes.*

More news now as MARWOOD *scans a rag. Here are*
murderers and muggers and photographs of tits and
advertisements for trusses and John and Yoko and
maniacal vicars and brassières and atomic bombs and
Vietnam and pillage and thousands on the rampage.

Wide-eyed with shock MARWOOD *lowers his*
newspaper. Practically everybody else in the dump is
behind one. This café is a hovel. Grease and fumes and
ketchup bottles with blackened foreskins. Some horrible
faces in here. MARWOOD *watches an old woman eating –*
her fried-egg sandwich ruptures. Loathing and fascination.
Loathing wins it and he turns away. Comes face to face
with 'Why I Did it – Mother of Eleven Tells All'. There is
no escape . . .

MARWOOD (V.O.): Thirteen million people have to cope
with this? And vicars and All Bran and rape? And I'm
sitting in this fucking shack and I can't cope with
Withnail? I must be out of my mind. I must go home
at once and discuss his problems in depth.

8. INT. STAIRWAY/LIVING ROOM. APARTMENT. DAY.
MARWOOD *blunders upstairs. Passes the bathroom door on his way. As he does so a man appears. Thirty years old. Pale as an oven-ready chicken. His hair is wet. The eyes have practically vanished under mauve lids. But the face is shaved and has dignity. So do the clothes. He wears a tweed overcoat. Corduroy trousers and brogues. There's class here somewhere. His name is* WITHNAIL.
WITHNAIL: I have some extremely distressing news . . .

> *His voice has been to Oxford and is deadly with sincerity.*

MARWOOD: I don't wanna hear it. I don't wanna hear anything.

> *Back to the living room. Nothing has changed except that it's now* filled *with steam. Neither seems to notice and* MARWOOD *doesn't remember he put a kettle on. He hot-foots it in and the pacing recommences. This time with an intensity that forewarns some sort of crisis.*

MARWOOD: My God, it's a nightmare out there. I tell you, it's a fucking nightmare.
WITHNAIL: We've just run out of wine. What are we gonna do about it?
MARWOOD: I dunno. I don't know. I don't feel good. I feel like my liver just stopped.

> MARWOOD'*s glasses mist with condensation. He pounds up the carpet wringing anxiety out of his newspaper . . . sees his reflection in a mirror. Muscles earthquake and he gets a rush.*

MARWOOD: Jesus Christ. I think I've overdone it. I think I've overdosed. My thumbs have gone weird. I'm in the middle of a fucking overdose . . .

WITHNAIL: Give me that newspaper . . .

He grabs the paper and collapses on the sofa.
MARWOOD *is still going up a hill.*

MARWOOD: . . . my heart's beating like a fucked clock. I feel dreadful. I feel fucking dreadful . . .

WITHNAIL: So do I. So does everybody. Look at my tongue. It's wearing a yellow sock. Sit down, for Christ's sake. What's the matter with you? Eat some sugar.

He fights the newspaper into shape. MARWOOD *gathers his senses and quicks it into the kitchen. Begins a frenzied search for a drinking receptacle. There's only a soup bowl. He's transferring sugar when* WITHNAIL *appears through the steam.*

WITHNAIL: Listen to this. 'Curse of the Supermen . . .'

WITHNAIL *is reading from the paper with a disturbing looking grin.*

'I took drugs to win medal, says top athlete, Jeff Wode.'

MARWOOD: Where's the coffee?

WITHNAIL: 'In a world exclusive interview, thirty-three year-old shot putter, Jeff Wode, who weighs three hundred and seventeen pounds, admitted taking massive doses of anabolic steroids, drugs banned in sport.'

MARWOOD *doesn't want to listen. Tangents off looking for coffee.*

'He used to get in bad tempers and act daft, says his wife. He used to pick on me. Now he's stopped, he's much better in our sex life, and in our general life.'

A jar of Maxwell House on the table. MARWOOD *grabs it and they return to the kitchen. Wode has excited* WITHNAIL*'s imagination.*

7

Jesus Christ, this huge thatched head with its
sideboards and cannon ball is now considered sane.
Jeff Wode is feeling better. And is now prepared to
step back into society and start tossing his orb about.

MARWOOD *shakes coffee from the jar and mixes it
with his finger. Grabbing a magazine he uses it to
insulate the white-hot kettle.*

Look at him. Look at Jeff Wode.

MARWOOD *pours water into the soup bowl. Is forced
to look at a face with hair sprouting from the nose
and ears – sideboards exiting from the nostrils.*

His ear lobes must weigh a pound and a half each . . .

MARWOOD: Take him away. I don't wanna see him.

WITHNAIL: Imagine the size of his balls.

> *The kettle returns to the gas. Jeff Wode is fascinating*
> WITHNAIL.

Imagine getting into a fight with the fucker.

Clutching his soup bowl MARWOOD *pushes past into
the living room.*

MARWOOD: Please. I don't feel good.

WITHNAIL: That's what you'd say. But that wouldn't wash
with *Jeff.* He'd like a bit of pleading. Adds spice to it.
In fact, he'd probably tell you what he was gonna do
before he did it. 'I'm gonna *pull your head off.*' 'No,
please. Please don't pull my head off.' 'I'm gonna *pull
your head off*, because I don't *like* your head . . .'

> WITHNAIL *stops mid-sentence. Stares with accelerating
> indignation.*

Have you got soup?

> MARWOOD *sits and begins sipping coffee from the
> edge of his bowl.*

Why don't I get any soup?

MARWOOD: Coffee.

WITHNAIL: Well why don't you use a *cup* like any other human being?

MARWOOD: Why don't you *wash up* occasionally like any other human being?

Before the words have left his mouth MARWOOD *realises he's made a mistake. If it is possible for a face as white as* WITHNAIL's *to pale the moment is now. Crumpling his newspaper he marches forward. In the interests of safety* MARWOOD *rises to his feet.*

WITHNAIL: How dare you? How *dare* you? How dare you call *me* inhumane?

MARWOOD: I didn't call you inhumane. You merely imagined that. Calm down.

WITHNAIL: Right you *fucker*. I'm gonna do the washing up. *The crisis has focused.* MARWOOD *moves in to prevent a development.*

MARWOOD: You can't. It's impossible. I swear to you. I've looked into it.

A cross between a scuffle and a waltz. MARWOOD *leading in both.*

Listen to me. *Listen.* There are *things* in there. There's a tea bag growing. You haven't slept for sixty hours, you're in no state to tackle it. Wait for the morning, and we'll go in together.

WITHNAIL: This *is* the morning. Stand aside.

Rolling up the sleeve of his overcoat WITHNAIL *barges into the steam.* MARWOOD *follows, issuing warnings.*

MARWOOD: You don't understand. I think there may be something *living* in there. I think there's something *alive* . . .

9

It's difficult to see what's happening. But WITHNAIL *is in possession of the Fairy Liquid bottle and is wielding it like a gun.*

WITHNAIL: What d'you mean, a *rat*?

MARWOOD: Possibly. It's possible.

WITHNAIL: Then the *fucker* will *rue* the *day*.

Firing his bottle WITHNAIL *plunges at the sink. Both taps go on and there's a clatter of activity.*

Christ Almighty.

And he staggers back clutching a saucepan filled with pungent brown fluids.

Sinew in nicotine base.

A fascination for the unclean drives MARWOOD *towards the visuals.*

Keep back. Keep back. The entire sink's gone rotten. I don't know what's in here.

A space for the saucepan is cleared. MARWOOD *stares at it while* WITHNAIL *pours water from the kettle and envelops himself in a cloud of super-heated steam. A volcanic growl comes from the fog.*

Bellowing loudly, WITHNAIL *passes at speed with his hand in the air.*

MARWOOD: I told you. You've been bitten.

WITHNAIL: *Burnt. Burnt.* The fucking kettle's on fire.

MARWOOD: There's something floating up.

WITHNAIL paces back into the kitchen. A voice laced with revenge.

WITHNAIL: Fork it.

MARWOOD: No. No. I don't wanna touch it.

WITHNAIL: You must. You must. That shit'll bore through the glaze. We'll never be able to use the dinner service again.

He tugs at a drawer stuffed with domestic items.
Produces a tool.

Here. Get it with the pliers.

MARWOOD: No. No. Give me the gloves.

Rubber gloves are handed across. WITHNAIL *stares as they go on.*

WITHNAIL: That's right. Put on the gloves. Don't attempt anything without the gloves.

Defying the view MARWOOD *goes in. Starts probing into the depths.*

MARWOOD: There's a boiled egg in here.

WITHNAIL: This is too much to bear.

An explosion of stagnant chilli and he reels back from the sink.

What is it? What have you *found*?

MARWOOD: Matter.

WITHNAIL: *Matter*? Where's it coming from?

WITHNAIL*'s eyes prod as he forces himself forward for an exposé.*

MARWOOD: Don't come. Don't look. I'm dealing with it.

WITHNAIL: I think we've been in here too long. I feel unusual. I think we should go outside.

MARWOOD *is diving for the foundations. Half a loaf comes out. Then other things. Both are dumbstruck. There is nothing they can do. Very slowly the image begins to dissolve . . .*

MARWOOD (*V.O.*): . . . a Chinese take-away was the foundation to this pile of horror . . . One flattened ball of pork (which the inventor may, in wide-eyed innocence, have conceived as *sweet*) . . .

9. EXT. REGENT'S PARK. LONDON. DAY.

MARWOOD (V.O.): . . . but could not, in his wildest
Chinese nightmare, have appreciated what the addition
of the word *sour* might entail . . .

Black railings against mist. Drizzle clings to the trees.
This is a section of the park bordering on the zoo.
Half a dozen wolves are hanging about, looking pissed
off. As bored with looking at WITHNAIL *and*
MARWOOD *as the two men are bored with looking at*
them. WITHNAIL *and* MARWOOD *turn away and start*
walking down a path. Overcoats wrapped around
them and arms wrapped around the coats.

WITHNAIL: This is ridiculous. Look at me. I'm thirty in a
month. And I've got a *sole* flapping off my shoe.

MARWOOD: It'll get better. It has to . . .

WITHNAIL's expression is a mixture of vitamin-lack
and cynicism.

WITHNAIL: Easy enough for you to say 'lovey', you've had
an audition . . . Why can't I have an audition?

An audition? Can these two wrecks be actors?
Evidently they are.

It's ridiculous. I've been to drama school. I'm good looking.
I tell you, I've a fuck sight more talent than half the rubbish
that gets on television. Why can't I get on television?

MARWOOD *has clearly listened to this before. He turns*
away cold.

MARWOOD: I dunno. It'll happen . . .

WITHNAIL: Will it? That's what you say. The only
programme I'm likely to get on is the fucking news.

The assessment is probably correct. Unlikely anyone
would let WITHNAIL *loose in a television studio. Much*
less pay him to be there.

WITHNAIL: I tell you, I can't take much more of this, I'm
   going to crack.
MARWOOD: I'm in the same boat . . .
WITHNAIL: (*muttering*): Yeah, yeah.
   Conversation blows away in the wind.
WITHNAIL: I feel sick as a pike. I'm gonna have to sit
   down.

10. EXT. PIAZZA. REGENT'S PARK. DAY.
A church bell tolls somewhere. Misery times eight equals
Sunday. MARWOOD *is squinting at his reflection in a*
puddle. Like an Escher drawing. WITHNAIL *sits shivering*
on a bench like he's been there all night.
MARWOOD: You know what we should do . . .
   And he walks back to join WITHNAIL. *Sits when he*
   fancies it.
   I say, you know what we should do?
WITHNAIL: How can I possibly know what *we* should do?
   What should we do?
MARWOOD: Get out of it for a while. Get into the
   countryside and rejuvenate.
WITHNAIL: Rejuvenate? I'm in a *park* and I'm practically
   dead. What good's the countryside? What time is it?
MARWOOD: Eight.
WITHNAIL: Four hours to opening. God help us.
   WITHNAIL *adjusts his massive tartan scarf.*
   Have we got any embrocation?
MARWOOD: What for?
WITHNAIL To *rub on us* you fool. We can cover ourselves
   in Deep Heat and get up against a radiator. Keep
   ourselves alive till twelve.
WITHNAIL *suddenly spits with great violence. An oyster is*

13

born. He observes it in a great state of partial hypnosis.

Jesus. Look at that. Apart from a raw potato, that's the only solid to pass my lips in the last sixty hours. I must be ill.

11. INT. LIVING ROOM. APARTMENT. DAY.
The shutters are open and WITHNAIL *stares across to the partially demolished building opposite. The site is silent but has a giant crane sporting one of those huge iron bash-balls on the end of a chain.*

MARWOOD (V.O.): Even a stopped clock gives the right time twice a day, and for once I am inclined to believe Withnail is right . . .

WITHNAIL *looks unstable and grimy with the hue of wet cement. Wears his overcoat and a sock. Entire corpse smeared with embrocation . . .*

. . . we are indeed drifting into the arena of the unwell. What we need is harmony . . . fresh air and stuff like that . . .

MARWOOD *sits on the sofa. Smokes a cigarette and puts thoughts into a battered notebook.*

WITHNAIL: Wasn't much in the tube. There's nothing left for you.

He throws MARWOOD *the empty tube and draws his overcoat around him.*

MARWOOD: Why don't you ask your father for some money? If we had some money we could go away.

WITHNAIL: Why don't you ask *your* father? How can it be so cold in here? It's like *Greenland* in here. We've got to get some booze. It's the only solution to this intense cold.

14

Donning a boot WITHNAIL *begins to patrol. There is a distinct possibility the fuses are going to blow. Muscles are white molars are grinding. A wild look in his eyes. And he's put on the rubber gloves.*

Something's got to be done. We can't go on like this. I'm a *trained actor* reduced to the status of a *bum*. Look at us. Nothing that reasonable members of society demand as their rights. No fridges. No televisions. No phones.

MARWOOD *isn't really listening. Continues to write in his book.*

Much more of this, I'm gonna apply for Meals on Wheels.

MARWOOD: What happened to your cigar commercial?

WITHNAIL: That's what I wanna know. What happened to my *cigar commercial*? What's happened to my *agent*? The bastard must have died.

MARWOOD: September. It's a bad patch.

WITHNAIL: Rubbish. I haven't seen Gielgud down the Labour Exchange.

WITHNAIL *is beginning to look like some minor character from a nineteenth-century Russian novel. Withnailovich. Incidental to the plot.*

Why doesn't he retire? (*Grabs newspaper*). Look at this little bastard. 'Boy lands plum role for top Italian director.' Course he does. Probably on a tenner a day. And I know what for. Two pound ten a tit and a fiver for his arse . . .

MARWOOD *has had enough of it. Stubs his cigarette and walks away.* WITHNAIL *is becoming unusual. He follows into the kitchen. Looks with disgust at* MARWOOD *who's got a fork going into a honey pot.*

Muttering invective about the temperature WITHNAIL
*poles off for his clothes. A thought suddenly occurs
and he turns accusingly.*

WITHNAIL: Have you been at the controls?

MARWOOD: What are you talking about?

WITHNAIL: The *thermostats*. What have you *done* to
them?

MARWOOD: Haven't touched them.

WITHNAIL: Then why has my head gone numb?

Some sort of climax approaches.

I must have some booze. I *demand* to have some
booze.

*His eyes sweep the room. Home in on a can of
Ronsonol.*

MARWOOD: I wouldn't drink that if I was you.

WITHNAIL: Why not? Why not?

MARWOOD: Because I don't advise it. Even wankers on the
site wouldn't drink that. That's worse than meths.

WITHNAIL: Nonsense. This is a far superior drink to
meths. The wankers don't drink it because they can't
afford it.

*Levering the cap with his teeth he tears it off. The
mouth opens with a bilious cackle and throwing his
head back* WITHNAIL *downs the petrol in one. A
falsetto whine follows as he comes up fighting for air.*
MARWOOD *looks worried.*

Have we got any more?

MARWOOD *looks more worried. Shakes his head and
steps back. This drug-crazed fool in overcoat and
underpants seems poised to kill.*

Liar. What's in your tool box?

MARWOOD: We have nothing. Sit down.

16

WITHNAIL: Liar. You've got anti-freeze.

One comes on and one backs off. The latter with certain urgency.

MARWOOD: You bloody fool. You should never mix your drinks!

The joke is an accident. It stops WITHNAIL *in his tracks. This is evidently the funniest thing he's ever heard. Barking with hysteria he staggers forward. Suddenly he's down. He throws up on* MARWOOD's *shoes. However, we'll be spared visuals of this incident.*

Mercifully, all we'll see is his reaction. The victim may mutter 'Oh, God, no.' And on the other hand he may not. Some music gets in here. A single bleak electric guitar.

12. INT. KITCHEN. APARTMENT. DAY.

The music will continue until I tell it to stop. MARWOOD *has his boots on the kitchen table. He's scrubbed them and applies perfume. The door bell rings and he freezes. As he moves he knocks the essence of petunia all over his trousers! No time to swear because he's heading for the living room.* WITHNAIL *is stretched along the couch under his overcoat. He squints up with equal alarm.*

MARWOOD *crouches in the window. A wing mirror from a motor-bike is bolted to the balcony outside. It affords a view of the front step. A bald and affluent-looking man lurking.*

MARWOOD: It's him . . .

WITHNAIL: We're out . . .

MARWOOD: I know we are . . .

13. EXT. STREET. CAMDEN TOWN. DAY.
Not a lot has changed since MARWOOD *was last in the street. More people about. Mainly Irish wankers hanging about the tube station for no apparent reason. Too daft or too broke to care that it's past opening time. Though they both look utterly wasted, the chuck up seems to have improved* WITHNAIL. *He counts change as they scuttle along.*

WITHNAIL: All right, this is the plan. We'll get in there and get wrecked. Then we'll eat a *pork pie*. Then we'll go home and drop a couple of Surmontil 50s each. That means we'll miss out Monday, but come up smiling Tuesday morning.
Were this a new theory of evolution the answer would be the same.

MARWOOD: It's a good idea . . .

WITHNAIL: Nothing ever happens on Mondays. I hate bastard Mondays.

14. INT. MOTHER BLACK CAP. PUBLIC HOUSE. DAY.
This is an Irish pub. It's filling up in direct proportion to the emptying of the churches. The bar is full of men. Only two women in here and they look like men. Faces like rotten beetroots. One has a tuft of carrot-coloured hair. Everybody here has one thing in common. They have come in here to get drunk. It's a horrible place. Shit-coloured Formica. Carpet like the surface of a road. The atmosphere is rank with smoke and Irish accent. WITHNAIL *leads the way to the bar and is served at once.*

WITHNAIL: Two large gins. Two pints of cider. Ice in the cider.

WITHNAIL *sits on a stool.* MARWOOD *supports himself*

18

on the bar, fiddling in the ashtray and rediscovering a thought.

MARWOOD: If my father was loaded, I'd ask him for some money.

WITHNAIL: And if your father was my father, you wouldn't get it.

A packet of Gauloises comes out. And here come the pair of gins.

Chin. Chin.

These boys are purely medicinal. Down in one. On to the ciders. Enough time passes for them both to get through half a glass.

MARWOOD: What about what's his name?

MARWOOD is in the middle of a conversation that never started.

WITHNAIL: What about him?

MARWOOD: Why don't you give him a call?

WITHNAIL: What for?

MARWOOD gestures to a phone on the wall behind WITHNAIL's head. If WITHNAIL weren't so wasted he'd perhaps focus the conversation.

MARWOOD: Ask him about his house.

WITHNAIL: You want me to call what's his name and ask him about his house?

MARWOOD: Why not?

WITHNAIL: All right. What's his number?

MARWOOD is so spaced he has to think a moment before replying.

MARWOOD: I've no idea. I've never met him.

WITHNAIL: Neither have I. Who the *fuck* are you talking about?

MARWOOD: Your relative. With the house in the country.

WITHNAIL: Monty? Uncle Monty?

MARWOOD: That's him. That's the one. Get the Jag fixed up and spend a week in the country.

If the phone were any further away the chances would be slim. But WITHNAIL *can almost reach it without getting off his stool.*

WITHNAIL: All right. Give us a tanner, and I'll give him a bell.

If muscles worked MARWOOD *would smile. He pulls a ten bob note.*

MARWOOD: Get a couple more in. I'm going for a slash . . .

WITHNAIL *is putting in another order as* MARWOOD *makes his way across the bar. An enormous* WANKER *is sitting by the lavatory door. He's had a few. He's togged out in a Burton's and wearing size twelve black platformed boots. Obviously fashion conscious. As* MARWOOD *passes, he looks up.*

WANKER: Ponce.

MARWOOD *registers the address but doesn't acknowledge it. Navigates into the Gents' with no visible manifestations of terror.*

15. INT. GENTS' LAVATORIES. DAY.

MARWOOD (*V.O. and playback*): I could hardly piss straight with fear. Here was a man with three-quarters of an inch of brain who had taken a dislike to me. What had I done to offend him? I don't consciously offend big men like this. This one has a definite imbalance of hormone in him. Get any more masculine than him and you'd have to live up a tree.

MARWOOD *is approaching a swoon. He leans into the*

20

*wall manufacturing sweat. 'I FUCK ARSES' is etched
into the plaster with dedication. His senses capsize at
the implications of the threat.*

I fuck arses? Who fucks arses? Maybe *he* fucks arses.
Maybe he's written this in some moment of drunken
sincerity? I'm in considerable danger in here. I must
get out of here at once . . .

*Following his own advice he zips and beats it through
the door.*

16. INT. MOTHER BLACK CAP. PUBLIC HOUSE. DAY.
The pair of size twelve black platform boots are still in situ.
WANKER: Perfumed ponce.

    MARWOOD *keeps walking and arrives at the bar.*
    WITHNAIL *greets him with a puckered smile.*
WITHNAIL: You'll be pleased to hear, Monty has invited
    us for drinks . . .
MARWOOD: Balls to Monty. We're getting out.
WITHNAIL: Balls to Monty? I've just spent an hour
    flattering the bugger.

    Two pints have just appeared. WITHNAIL's *interest is
    with them.*
MARWOOD: There's one over there doesn't like the
    perfume. A big one.

    WITHNAIL *manipulates a mouthful of cider. Swallows
    it and turns.*
MARWOOD (*cont.*): Don't look, don't look. We're in
    danger. We gotta get out.
WITHNAIL: What are you talking about?
MARWOOD: I've been called a ponce.

    More pissed than sensible WITHNAIL *swivels boldly on
    the bar.*

21

WITHNAIL: What *fucker* said that?

The fucker who said it has just put full weight on to his size twelves. And they're coming across the room. Intuitively WITHNAIL realises this is him. A profound change in his expression.

This man is huge. Red hair. Face and neck peppered with stubble and bright red with drink. At the end of his arms are arguably the biggest hands in existence. Both bramble-patched with hair.

As the WANKER approaches WITHNAIL attempts to dissociate himself from MARWOOD. But the technique is totally unsuccessful and WITHNAIL faces the WANKER.

WANKER: I called him a ponce. And now I'm calling you one. Ponce.

WITHNAIL: Would you like a drink?

No he wouldn't. He's had ten pints. That's why he's over here. He grabs WITHNAIL's tartan scarf and renders it unto the floor.

WANKER: What's your name? McFuck?

A couple of days pass while WITHNAIL searches for a suitable reply.

WITHNAIL: I have a heart condition.

The bastard is working himself into some kind of violent lather.

I have a heart condition.

If you hit me it's murder.

WANKER: I'll murder the paira ya.

His eyes alternate between them. Pork ugly. Organs of a brute. WITHNAIL's voice comes out in a curiously high-pitched whisper.

WITHNAIL: My wife is having a baby.

Both WITHNAIL *and* MARWOOD *are paralysed with panic. Both are speechless with fear. They stand to attention in front of the* WANKER *like defendants awaiting sentence. Hoping for the best. Expecting a dose of knuckle.* WITHNAIL *composes himself.*

I don't know what my acquaintance did to upset you. But it was nothing to do with me . . .

Can WITHNAIL *really be saying this?* MARWOOD *is sweating adrenalin. His eyes are on the door. This has to be his only chance.*

I suggest you both go outside and discuss it sensibly in the street . . .

Precisely where MARWOOD *is heading. But* WITHNAIL *is through the door first. Bellowing.*

Get out of my way.

He sprints into the street. For one who can hardly stand, he moves at amazing speed. The solitary acid electric guitar gets involved again. Bursts out with them . . .

17. EXT. CAMDEN HIGH ROAD. DAY.

And runs with them over this fast track. Two hundred yards are covered at a hot foot. WITHNAIL *slightly in the lead. They arrive under the bridge and collapse gasping over railings.*

WITHNAIL: You could have grabbed the scarf. It was by your fucking feet . . .

18. INT. BATHROOM. APARTMENT. DAY.

This bathroom is a psychological deterrent to cleanliness. It is unclean. At some time in the past somebody has had an epileptic fit in here with a can of fluorescent paint. There is wet rot and dry rot. Evil-looking pustules are

breaking through. A poster of Laurence Olivier as Othello
clings to one of the walls.

MARWOOD (V.O.): Speed is like a dozen transatlantic
flights without ever getting off the plane. Time change.
You lose. You gain. Makes no difference so long as
you keep taking the pills . . .

*The room is very small. A lavatory at one end. A bath
at the other. The type you sit up in like a huge enamel
armchair. MARWOOD is sitting up in it. Pocked and
shocked and attempting to shave. He wears a Shetland
jumper rolled up to just under his armpits. This
obviously affords protection against the cold. A mirror
is propped behind the taps. His reflection appears in it.*

MARWOOD (V.O.): But some time or another you gotta
get out. Because it's crashing. And all at once those
frozen hours melt through the nervous system and seep
out the pores.

*He rinses the razor and shivers. WITHNAIL bursts in
wearing his overcoat.*

He clutches a couple of doses of fish and chips.

WITHNAIL: Bastards. Just to suck some miserable cheap
cigar, and the bastards won't see me.

He thrusts a greasy parcel of newspaper across.

MARWOOD *begins unwrapping it.* WITHNAIL *lowers
the toilet seat and sits to eat.*

MARWOOD: Why are we having lunch in here?

WITHNAIL: It's dinner. And Danny's here.

MARWOOD: Danny? How'd he get in?

WITHNAIL: I let him in this morning. He's lost one of his
clogs. He's come in because of this perpetual cold.

MARWOOD *seems concerned at the news. Produces an
orange sausage.*

24

WITHNAIL: I hope tobacco sales plummet.

MARWOOD: I've got your saveloy.

> WITHNAIL *stands. Pitches his fish and chips into the kazi and flushes it.*

I don't want it.

WITHNAIL: Then stick it in the soap tray and save it for later.

MARWOOD: Don't vent spleen on me. I'm in the same boat . . .

WITHNAIL: Stop *saying* that! You're not in the same boat! The only thing you're in that I've been in is this *fucking* bath.

> *He storms out muttering curses. Principally* 'They will suffer.' MARWOOD *lowers his chips. His eyes slip focus into the mirror.*

MARWOOD (*V.O. and playback*): Danny's here. Head-hunter to his friends. Head-hunter to everybody. He doesn't have any friends. The only people he converses with are his clients and occasionally the police. The purveyor of rare herbs and prescribed chemicals is back. Will we never be set free?

> *Focus continues to slip. Another face waits at the end of it.*

19. INT. KITCHEN. APARTMENT. DAY.

DANNY *is a man who kept the* News of the World *in business all through the 1960s. And at the end of them put* Oz *out of it. He has dedicated his adult life to drugs. And it shows. He is a wreck. About sixty except he's twenty-six. A jade streak in his hair and night-black shades. Get down, punks. This man is before you were born.*

> MARWOOD *walks in wrapped in a towel.* DANNY's

voice is cultured Cockney. Monotoned. And brain-bummed.

DANNY: You're lookin' very beautiful man. Have you been away?

MARWOOD shakes his head. Fills the kettle and gives it the gas.

St Peter preached the epistles to the apostles looking like that. Have you got any food?

MARWOOD: I've got a saveloy.

The item is handed across. DANNY examines it as though it were some kind of deal. Gives it a sniffing and decides he likes it.

DANNY: How much is it?

MARWOOD: You can have it for nothing.

DANNY returns to the living room to put it in his bag.

WITHNAIL hobbles in re-togged in a tweed suit. It's old but has quality. Possibly came from a will. DANNY looks across with curiosity.

DANNY: I see you're wearin' a suit.

WITHNAIL: What's it gotta do with you?

One of WITHNAIL's boots is on the table. Matchsticks separate the sole from the uppers. A cobbling operation is in progress.

DANNY: No need to get uptight man. I was merely makin' an observation.

He slumps on the sofa. WITHNAIL carefully adjusts a paisley tie. I happened to be lookin' for a suit for the Coalman two weeks ago . . .

DANNY conducts an audit of the ashtray. Finds a suitable butt.

For reasons I can't really discuss with you, the

Coalman had to go to Jamaica, and got busted comin'
back through Heathrow . . .

WITHNAIL *puts his boot on and stands on it to secure
adhesion.*

Had a weight under his Fez . . .

Half an inch of Gauloise is lit. WITHNAIL *pipes 'Make
us a cup.'*

DANNY: We worked out it would be handykarma for him
to get hold of a suit. But he's a very low temperature
spade, the Coalman. Goes in in his kaftan and a
bell . . .

*The Gauloise produces a single cough before it takes a
stubbing.*

This doesn't go down at all well. They can handle the
kaftan. They can't handle the bell. So there's this judge
sittin' there in a cape like fuckin' Bat Man, with this
re-ally rather far-out lookin' hat . . .

WITHNAIL: A wig.

DANNY: No man. This was more like a long white hat.
And he looks at the Coalman and says, what's all this?
This is a court man, this ain't fancy-dress. So the
Coalman looks at him, and he says, 'You think you
look normal, your honour?' And the cunt gives him
two years . . .

MARWOOD *comes in with a couple of cups. Hands
one to* WITHNAIL.

I'm afraid I can't offer you gentlemen anything . . .

MARWOOD: That's all right, Danny. We decided to lay off
for a bit.

DANNY: That's what I thought. 'Cept for personal use, I
concur with you. As a mattera fact, I'm thinkina
retirin' and goin' inta business.

WITHNAIL: Doing what?

DANNY: The toy industry.

> WITHNAIL *gestures to a small, pink child's hot-water bottle on the sofa. It's connected to straps and sprouts a yard of plastic pipe.*

WITHNAIL: I thought you were in the bottle industry?

> MARWOOD *glances at the contraption and starts assembling clothes.*

DANNY: No man. That's a sideline. You can have that. Instructions are included.

> *Nobody pays it any attention.* WITHNAIL *decreases the pressure.*

Yeah, my partner's got an idea for makin' dolls. His name's Presuming Ed. His sister give him the idea. She got a doll on Christmas what pisses itself.

MARWOOD: Really?

DANNY: Yeah. Then you gotta change its drawers for it. S'horrible really, but they like that, the little girls. So we're gonna make one that shits itself as well . . .

WITHNAIL: Shits itself?

DANNY: He's an expert. He's buildin' the prototype now.

> WITHNAIL *decides to give his boot a test run. Makes a couple of journeys to the kitchen and back.*

DANNY: Why is he behavin' so uptightly?

WITHNAIL: Because a gang of cheeroot vendors considered a haircut beyond the limit of my abilities . . .

DANNY: I don't advise a haircut man. All hairdressers are in the employment of the government. Hairs are your aerials. They pick up signals from the cosmos, and transmit them directly into the brain. This is the reason bald-headed men are uptight.

WITHNAIL: What absolute twaddle.

WITHNAIL *disguises glue with polish.* MARWOOD *gets into a shirt.*

DANNY: Has he just been busted?

No he hasn't. MARWOOD *focuses into a mirror. Also wearing a tie.*

Then why's he wearin' that old suit?

WITHNAIL: Old suit? This suit was cut by Hawke's of Savile Row. Just because the best tailoring you've ever seen is above your fucking appendix doesn't mean anything.

DANNY: Don't get uptight with me man. 'Cause, if you do, I'll have to give you a dose of medicine. And if I spike you, you'll know you've been spoken to.

WITHNAIL: You wouldn't spike me. You're too mean. Anyway, there's nothing invented I couldn't take.

This is dangerous talk. MARWOOD *is beginning to look concerned.*

DANNY: If I medicined you, you'd think a brain tumour was a birthday present.

WITHNAIL: I could take *double* anything you could.

There is a very long pause. The apothecary rolls a tongue over his contaminated teeth. Takes his glasses off and somehow manages to lower an eye in his head. He may be smiling. If Fritz Lang were alive he'd be a star.

DANNY: Very, very foolish words man.

There's a confrontation coming. MARWOOD *moves in to defuse it.*

MARWOOD: He's right, Withnail. Don't be a fool. Look at him, his mechanism's gone. He's taken more drugs than you've had hot dinners.

WITHNAIL: I'm not having this shag-sack insulting me. Let him get his drugs out . . .

WITHNAIL *watches with a supercilious leer as* DANNY
*empties his shopping bag. Horrible things in it. Food
remains. Dead flowers. A bottle of nail varnish. And a
rubber doll. Perhaps the prototype? He holds it
menacingly at* WITHNAIL

DANNY: This doll is extremely dangerous. It has voodoo
   qualities.
   WITHNAIL *sniggers at it. Enrages its owner. Its bald
   and ugly little head is torn off and its guts emptied on
   to the table. Two dozen coloured spansules. A dozen
   soiled and assorted pills.* DANNY *sifts through isolating
   a tiny pink tablet. He looks up at* WITHNAIL *as
   though this item prevents all further argument.*

DANNY: Trade – phenodihydrochloride – benzorex. Street
   – the embalmer.

WITHNAIL: Balls. I'll swallow it and run a mile.
   WITHNAIL *reaches for it. A khaki finger detains it
   where it is.*

DANNY: Cool your boots man. This pill's valued at two
   quid.

WITHNAIL: Two quid? You're outa your mind.

MARWOOD: That's sense, Withnail.

WITHNAIL: You can stick it up your arse for nothing, and
   fuck off while you're doing it.

DANNY: No need to insult me man. I was leavin' anyway.
   *He gathers his equipment and stands. Slings a pelt
   around him.*
   Have either of you got shoes?

20. EXT. CHELSEA EMBANKMENT. EVENING.
*Moisture puts the city out of focus. The Jaguar speeds
along the Embankment. One headlight is functioning on*

the driver's side, one windscreen wiper on the passenger's.
The car turns into a crescent of imposing Victorian houses.
Pulls up and the pair of them get out.

WITHNAIL *checks his sole before crossing the road.*
MARWOOD *follows straightening his trousers. Parked*
opposite is a huge Sedanca Rolls. 1948 and immaculate.
WITHNAIL *looks approvingly as they pass. This is*
'Monty's car'.

21. INT. HALLWAY/CHELSEA HOUSE. EVENING.
A brass lion's head knocker goes into operation. Here's a
sight. A wall of Mozart with UNCLE MONTY *standing in*
front of it. He holds a cat in his right hand and a glass
teapot filled with water in his left. He's delighted to see
them. With a rococo sweep of the dangling cat he ushers
them in and the coats come off. MONTY *is large with a*
reptilian quality. His nose dominates the face and is the
colour of port. Somehow his head has managed to grow
round his glasses like trees grow round wire. In his lapel is
a radish the same colour as his nose.
MONTY: Sit down. Do. Would you like a drink?
MARWOOD *puts in for a gin and tonic and* WITHNAIL
for a sherry. WITHNAIL *is obviously to be taken*
seriously. There's a trolley full of malt whisky here so
he is out to make a good impression. Paintings and
tapestries decorate the walls.
MARWOOD *is somewhat uncomfortable in these*
surroundings. In complete contrast WITHNAIL *is totally*
at ease. Apart from the magnificent furniture the room
is filled with vegetables. Cauliflowers and carrots are
on every surface in valuable antique pots. A silver tray
on the table sprouts a dozen fully grown onions. In the

31

bay window is a fucking great cabbage, the size of an aspidistra. MARWOOD *is staring at its luxurious foliage when* UNCLE MONTY *pirouettes in with the drinks.*

MONTY: Do you like vegetables?

MARWOOD nods and MONTY *wafts dust from the leaves of a parsnip.*

I've always been fond of root crops, but I only started to grow last summer . . .

MONTY *proffers glasses and* WITHNAIL *moves in for a* 'Chin chin'.

I happen to think the cauliflower more beautiful than the rose.

He moves off at speed towards a turnip in an art nouveau *pot.*

Do you grow?

WITHNAIL: Geraniums . . .

News to MARWOOD. MONTY *swings towards him. Exchange of smiles.*

MONTY: You little traitors. I think the carrot infinitely more fascinating than the geranium. The carrot has mystery. Flowers are essentially tarts. Prostitutes for the bees . . .

All this is said isolating MARWOOD. *He returns an uneasy smile.* MONTY *evaporates into the kitchen with a giggle towards* WITHNAIL.

Help yourselves to another drink.

WITHNAIL *immediately leaps to his feet and downs several huge gulps of whisky from the bottle. Corks it quickly and refills his glass with more sherry.*

MARWOOD *is whispering in concern.*

MARWOOD: What's all this? The man's mad.

WITHNAIL: Eccentric.

MARWOOD: Eccentric? He's insane. Not only that, he's a
raving homosexual . . .

*They reseat at speed and attempt to look relaxed. The
cat comes skidding out, followed by* MONTY *with a
purple face. He lumbers after it with veins throbbing.*

MONTY: Beastly little parasite. How dare you? You little
thug. How dare you?

A degree of surprise from the assembled as MONTY
*goes after the mog. It shelters behind a leek and he
concedes to its agility. Wiping sweat from his brow*
MONTY *calms and sits next to* MARWOOD.

MONTY: Beastly ungrateful little swine . . .

WITHNAIL: Shall I get you a drink, Monty?

A crimson silk handkerchief returns to MONTY's
breast pocket.

MONTY: Yes, yes, yes please dear boy. You can prepare
me a small rhesus-negative Bloody Mary. And you
must tell me all the news. I haven't seen you since you
finished the last film . . .

And MARWOOD's *certain he hasn't seen the first
either.*

WITHNAIL: Rather busy, Uncle . . . TV and stuff. And my
agent's attempting to edge me towards the Royal
Shakespeare Company again.

MONTY: Splendid.

WITHNAIL: And he's just had an audition for rep.

MONTY: Oh splendid. So you're a thesbian too?

MARWOOD *is not a little taken aback by the word
'thesbian'.*

WITHNAIL: Monty used to act.

MONTY: Oh, I'd hardly say that. It's true I crept the

boards in my youth. But I never really had it in my blood . . . and that's what's so essential, isn't it? Theatrical zeal in the veins? Alas, I have little more than vintage wine and memories.

And one of them is on the crowded mantelpiece. A photograph of Monty in his youth. A sepia reminiscence in a doublet and hose. He stands and almost clasps it. A dose of mothballs and Adelphi. It is the most shattering experience of a young man's life, when one morning he awakes, and quite reasonably says to himself, I will *never* play the Dane. When that moment comes, one's ambition ceases . . . *He turns back towards* MARWOOD, *his voice sonorous with emotion.*

Don't you agree?

WITHNAIL: It's a part I intend to play, Uncle.

MONTY: And you'd be *marvellous* . . . marvellous . . .

MONTY is suddenly on the ramparts. Whispering at the Ghost he never saw. Now located somewhere towards the ceiling of the apartment. MARWOOD has had enough of this. Moves on WITHNAIL with a whisper.

MARWOOD: Let's get out of here . . . come on. He's a madman. Any minute now he's gonna rush out and get into his tights.

WITHNAIL: OK. OK. Gimme a minute.

MARWOOD: The house, or out.

WITHNAIL is persuaded and approaches MONTY who turns dew-eyed.

WITHNAIL: Could I have a word with you Monty?

MONTY: Forgive me, forgive me. I was allowing memory to have the better of me. Seeing you boys, so young,

so filled with the fire of the theatre, puts a sting of
nostalgia into one's nose . . .

WITHNAIL *agrees and manoeuvres him to the sofa.*
MARWOOD *wanders into the Mozart as* WITHNAIL
*hits the old bastard with a sherry. Too much music
and too far away to hear what is said. But* WITHNAIL
is in full-throated ease. MARWOOD *examines a table
infected with silver-framed photographs. One of a little
boy sitting on the running board of a vintage Bentley.
Monty is at the wheel. The little boy in the straw hat
is clearly Withnail.* WITHNAIL *is suddenly on his feet
and heading for the drinks. He shoots a glance at*
MARWOOD. *Evidently pulled it off. The house is in the
bag.* MARWOOD *is delighted and drifts back into the
conversation.*

MONTY: Indeed, I remember my first agent. Raymond
Duck. He was a dreadful little Israelite. Four floors up
on the Charing Cross Road and never a job at the top
of them . . .

WITHNAIL *is pouring whisky. Confident he has landed
his fish.* MONTY *redirects eyes to a hovering*
MARWOOD.

I'm told you are a writer too.

MARWOOD *can't find any reaction here but a shrug
and a smile.*

Do you write poems?

MARWOOD: No, I wish I could. Just thoughts, really.
MONTY: Are you published?
MARWOOD: Oh no.
MONTY: Where did you school?

WITHNAIL *takes a sudden interest in the conversation
and says:*

WITHNAIL: He went to the other place, Monty.

MARWOOD *doesn't know what the 'other place' is.*
MONTY *does and is launching into a sentence
beginning,* 'Oh, you went to Eton . . .' *when
something terrible happens. At this most crucial stage
in the negotiations the cat reappears. For reasons best
known to itself it throws itself at* WITHNAIL. MONTY
*rears to his feet driving the already dangerous levels of
blood pressure into the capillaries of his swollen conk.*

MONTY: Get that damned little swine out of here. It's
trying to get itself in with you. Trying for even more
advantage. It's obsessed with its gut. It's like a bloody
rugby ball now.

Swinging his arms wildly he makes towards WITHNAIL
*and his cat in a menacing stoop. Both manage to get
out of his way. Snorting oaths the uncle follows the
animal to a corner where it snarls in horror.* MONTY
swivels seeking to cut off escape. MARWOOD *and*
WITHNAIL *watch in amazement as pursuit continues.*
MONTY *lumbers through his tray of onions and the
cat suddenly vanishes.*

It will die. It will die.

WITHNAIL *takes his arm and manages to escort him to
the sofa.*

WITHNAIL: Let me get you a top up . . .

Ill-charted maps of the Orinoco delta throb in
MONTY'*s temples.*

MONTY: No, dear boy, you must leave, you must leave.
Yet again that oaf has destroyed my day.

Everything is slipping away. MARWOOD *doesn't seem
to care any more. Despite all work put in with this
raving aberration he is prepared to leave instantly. So*

it seems is WITHNAIL. *Then a thought. And a change of gear.*

WITHNAIL: Listen, Monty, could I just have a quick word with you in private?
MONTY looks at him, preparing to say no. But WITHNAIL *is earnest. Groaning* 'Very well,' *he allows himself to be shunted towards a bedroom.*
MARWOOD *has no idea what the plan is. But even so isn't entirely happy with it. He stares after them till the door shuts.*

On the instant the cat reappears displaying the stealth that secures its existence in such uncongenial lodgings. MARWOOD *eyes it with vague animosity. But the thing is no longer of importance. Finishing his whisky he finds himself back at the windows. Night and lights and mist on the river.*

Any more of this and it's art.

MARWOOD (V.O.): How many more maniacs out there? Nurturing their turnips. Living in greenhouses with paranoid cats terrified by the sonnets of the Bard? Possibly thousands. Those with the money are eccentric. Those without. Insane.
The door suddenly opens. MONTY *out first. Considerably mellowed and showing stabilisation of blood pressure.* WITHNAIL *out next. Doesn't meet* MARWOOD's *eyes but walks straight into the hall for his coat.* MARWOOD *swaps a smile with* MONTY *and they vanish into an entrance hall.*

22. INT. ENTRANCE HALL. HOUSE. NIGHT.
A huge red-pepper plant and a bust of a boy. MARWOOD *is glad to be out but vaguely ill at ease.*

MARWOOD: Whass all this going off in private business?
    WITHNAIL *answers with an enigmatic and annoying*
    smile.

    Why'd you tell him I went to Eton?
WITHNAIL: Because it wouldn't have helped if I hadn't. I
    was just trying to establish you in some sort of context
    he'd understand . . .
MARWOOD: What d'you mean by that?
    The elevator arrives and WITHNAIL *leads the way in.*
    A smug smile on his kisser a large iron key dangling
    from his finger.
WITHNAIL: I mean, *free* to those that can afford it, *very*
    expensive to those that can't.

23. INT. SERVICE PIT. GARAGE. DAY.
A greasy little back-street dungeon. The Jaguar is shoulder
height on a hydraulic jack. WITHNAIL *and* MARWOOD
watch while a weaselish MECHANIC *pokes beneath it with*
a naked 100-watt bulb in a little wire cage. Doesn't like
the look of what he sees. Stubbing his butt he emerges to
address MARWOOD.
MECHANIC: Bob or two either sida forty quid.
MARWOOD: Forty quid? If we had forty quid, we'd buy a
    better car.
MECHANIC: This thing's unroadworthy. I've seen better
    tyres hanging over the side of a tug.
WITHNAIL: Nonsense. It's in first-class condition. Right,
    get it down, we'll service it ourselves.

24. EXT. GARAGE FORECOURT. DAY.
And the shot cranes down. Music and a bit of drizzle
about. The Jag rumbles in and they dismount. WITHNAIL

opens the boot, shouting mechanical instructions at
MARWOOD.

WITHNAIL: Right, you service the water and I'll service the
 tyres. Then you can service the battery, and then we'll
 go home and get under the sink.
 An air hose and a watering can. A free service and a
 slow dissolve which the music survives.

25. INT. KITCHEN. APARTMENT. DAY.

WITHNAIL *is arse out on his knees in the cupboard under*
the sink. A forest of bottles surrounds him. Regiments of
Guinness and Bass. MARWOOD *is computing their value*
with a pad and pencil. The last bottle comes out and
WITHNAIL *stands and prepares for the total.*

MARWOOD: I make it a tanner under four quid.

WITHNAIL: All right, let's work this out. Three pounds
 nineteen and six, plus thirteen pounds three and nine
 National Assistance, plus your thirty-two quid three
 and four, that makes fifty pounds six and seven.

MARWOOD: Does it?

WITHNAIL: I've just said so, haven't I. Right, at eight and
 eleven a bottle, that means we can have ninety-six
 bottles of Greek Hock.

MARWOOD: Ninety-six bottles of Greek Hock? You're out
 of your fucking mind.
 WITHNAIL *starts loading the empties.* MARWOOD
 counts the money.

WITHNAIL: I'm not suggesting we spend the entire amount
 on Greek Hock. We'll have nine two-and-a-half litres
 of Eye-tie red and three dozen barley wines . . .

MARWOOD: How much is that?

26. INT. OFF LICENCE. DAY.

A horrible pinstripe suit. Dandruff. This is their wine BROKER. *And they're broke. And this is his wine. And* WITHNAIL'*s pissed.*

BROKER: Fifteen pounds twelve and a penny.

WITHNAIL: Good. We'll have a bottle of Haig.

> *The* BROKER *goes about it.* MARWOOD *is unhappy with the last item.*

MARWOOD: Don't be an idiot. We can't afford it.

> *The whisky joins the wine. The* BROKER *observes without comment.*

WITHNAIL: You've had petrol. I want whisky.

MARWOOD: *I've* had petrol? We've *both* had petrol.

WITHNAIL: You've had *oil*.

MARWOOD: *Of course* I've had oil! It's four hundred miles . . .

WITHNAIL: I'm not sitting in that wreck all night without whisky. It's essential.

> *He moves for the bottle – arm on same plane as the wrecking ball.*

27. EXT. DEMOLITION SITE/STREET. CAMDEN TOWN. DAY.

Mr Hendrix plays Mr Dylan's 'All Along the Watch Tower'. This music will choreograph the journey north. The music starts here. Violence on electric guitar. Violence in the street. That fucking great demolition ball is in action. Puts one into the belly of a wall and it collapses like a drunk. Much rubble and dust. As it draws back for another blow the camera moves with it and keeps moving on to the Jag. WITHNAIL *already inside with his bottle of whisky.* MARWOOD *gets into the driving seat. He wears*

*clip-on shades on his glasses. He starts the car and glances
across at the site. With one finger he flicks the shades
down. The car disappears under the bridge.*

28. EXT. STREET. SUBURBS. LONDON. DAY.
*The music heads north with the Jaguar through the
wastelands of Finchley and Hendon. A scrag land of TV
aerials and faces in corporate shock. Miles and miles of
recently constructed high-rise slums. Each with its
architecturally designed and resident-vandalised tree.*

*A roar from the twin punctured exhausts. They pass a
line of schoolgirls at a bus stop.* WITHNAIL *hanging from
his window.*

WITHNAIL: *Scrubbers. Scrubbers.*

29. INT. JAG SEDAN. DAY.
WITHNAIL *clasps the Haig. Laughing out and pissed as a
gorilla.*

MARWOOD: Shut up . . .

WITHNAIL: Little tarts. They love it . . .

MARWOOD: Listen to me. I'm trying to drive this thing as
    quietly as possible. If you don't shut up, we're gonna
    get stopped by the police. Gimme the bottle.
    MARWOOD *grabs the whisky. Takes a hit.* WITHNAIL
    *grabs it back. Another guzzle at the bottle. And
    another exterior attraction. They pass a sign:*
    'ACCIDENT BLACK SPOT. DRIVE WITH EXTREME CARE.
    LONDON BOROUGH OF FINCHLEY.'

WITHNAIL: Look at that! Look at that! Accident black
    spot! These aren't *accidents.* They're *throwing
    themselves into the road!* Gladly! Throwing themselves
    into the road to escape all this hideousness.

41

A yob on a corner. The window goes down again.
WITHNAIL *screams.*
Throw yourself into the road, darling. You haven't got a chance.
The car vanishes into a perspective of street and exhaust fumes.

30. EXT. MI. MOTORWAY ENTRANCE RAMP. DAY.
The Jag is giving its ninety. Brutal rust on a traffic-free road.

31. EXT. MI. MOTORWAY. EVENING.
Factories and power stations and morbid industrial complexes. The land is in ruins and so is the sky. Great greasy clouds are piling on the horizon. It'll be dark in less than an hour.
WITHNAIL (V.O.): At some time or another, I wanna stop and get hold of a child . . .
MARWOOD (V.O.): What d'you want a child for?
WITHNAIL (V.O.): To tutor it in the ways of righteousness, and procure some uncontaminated urine.

32. INT. JAGUAR SEDAN. EVENING.
WITHNAIL *is unravelling plastic hose from the hot-water bottle. Trying to work out where the strings and straps should be. Gets the bottle under an armpit and starts waving some sort of valve.*
WITHNAIL: This is a device enabling the drunken driver to operate in absolute safety. You fill it with piss, take this pipe down the trouser, and Sellotape this valve to the end of the old chap. Then you get horribly drunk, and they can't fucking touch you.

MARWOOD *glances across. An instruction sheet takes*
an unfolding.

WITHNAIL: According to these instructions, you refuse
everything but a urine sample. You undo your valve,
give 'em a dose of unadulterated child's piss, and they
have to give you your keys back.

WITHNAIL *takes another large slug of whisky. So does*
MARWOOD.

WITHNAIL: Danny's a genius. I'm gonna have a doze.

33. EXT. MI. MOTORWAY. EVENING.
Bridges and other roadside bollocks. The Jaguar thunders
past.

34. EXT. MOTORWAY INTERSECTION. DEEP EVENING.
A scraping of daylight left. Headlight on the Jag swings off
the motorway on to a minor road. Going to piss down any
minute now.

35. EXT. COUNTRY ROAD. VALLEY. DEEPER EVENING.
The Jaguar hits the rain. Hardly any decrease in speed.
Black and ominous-looking hills. Balls of black cloud
rolling into a valley. The car descends with them. The
brake lights come on, and the music ends.

36. EXT. COUNTRY ROAD. NIGHT.
MARWOOD *pulls over and climbs out. One hell of a*
gale is blowing. He gets to the passenger side of the car.
Starts wrenching at the still-moving wiper blade.
WITHNAIL's *face is periodically visible. Wrecked in his*
seat and asleep with his jaw wide open. MARWOOD *fails*
to relocate the wiper blade. Soaking wet and furious he

staggers back to his door. Slams it with nothing achieved.

37. INT. JAGUAR SEDAN. NIGHT.
The force of MARWOOD's *entry wakes his co-pilot and navigator. Nothing but the beat of the windscreen wiper.*

WITHNAIL: Are we there?

MARWOOD: No we're not. We're here. And we're in the middle of a fucking gale.

He starts the engine and pulls out. Snaps instructions at WITHNAIL.

You'll have to keep a lookout your side. If you see anything, tell me. And get holda that map.

WITHNAIL *emits an accelerating groan. Something to do with a headache. He looks across. Eyes like a pair of decayed clams.*

WITHNAIL: Where's the whisky?

MARWOOD: What for?

WITHNAIL: I got a bastard behind the eyes. I can't take aspirins without a drink . . .

The bottle is discovered. The cork popped. And back to MARWOOD.

Where's the aspirins?

MARWOOD: Probably in the bathroom.

WITHNAIL: You mean we've come out here in the middle of fucking nowhere without aspirins?

This appears to be the case. WITHNAIL *is becoming emotional.*

MARWOOD: Where are we?

WITHNAIL: How should I know where we are? I feel like a pig shat in my head.

44

MARWOOD: Get hold of that map, and look for a place
    called Crow Crag.
WITHNAIL: I can't. I've gone blind. My bladder's
    exploding. I've got to have a slash.
MARWOOD: You can't have one.
    MARWOOD *is nearly in* WITHNAIL's *lap trying to see
    some road.*
WITHNAIL: What do you mean I *can't* have one? I've *got*
    to have one. Stop this bastard and let me out.
MARWOOD: No. Look at the map. Find a biro cross.
    WITHNAIL *grabs it. Practically destroys it. Approaches
    a shout.*
WITHNAIL: We're about a *yard* from London, and going
    up a hill! Now, for Christ's sake, stop this crate and
    let me out.

38. EXT. COUNTRY ROAD. NIGHT.
*The night is overpoweringly black. Towards the end of his
monumentally long piss* WITHNAIL *turns to* MARWOOD.
WITHNAIL: I think all this is a mistake. A serious and
    soon-to-be-regretted mistake.

39. EXT. COUNTRYSIDE. NIGHT.
The Jag winds up a maze of stone walls.
    *The Jag passes a concealed entrance. Backs up to reveal
a sign saying Crow Crag Farm. Takes this turning.*
    *The car passes through Crow Crag Farm and continues.
    The Jaguar bumps down a rutted track in deep night.*
    WITHNAIL's *P.O.V. interior car. Windscreen wiper
battling the rain. A house comes into view.*
    *Above the car as its single headlight sweeps a bleak-
looking cottage.*

At a glance picturesque. Mud conspires to prevent
MARWOOD's *sharp right-angled turn into the yard. The*
car slides into the gate. A crank of a handbrake and they
get out.
WITHNAIL: There must and shall be aspirin . . .

> MARWOOD *levers a pair of suitcases and grocery bags*
> *from the car. Violent rain sweeps through the single*
> *headlight.*
> WITHNAIL *hangs over the partially open gate like laundry.*
> If I don't get aspirin, I shall die, here, on this fucking
> mountainside.

Staggers, groaning, to the front and gets pushed aside.
MARWOOD: Give me the key. And get outta the way.

40. INT. COTTAGE. NIGHT.
The door opens, revealing a smudge of headlight from
outside. MARWOOD *strikes a match and* WITHNAIL
whispers, 'Christ Almighty.' In the instant before the
match goes out they see crumbling walls and stale shadows
and giant atlases of damp on the floor. They also see an
oil lamp. The match goes out. Another one is lit. A yellow
glow and the lamp reveals all. Table with several chairs.
Old but not antique. A photograph of a football team. All
with moustaches and shorts down to their knees. 'Oxford
1926.' Is one of them Monty? Two armchairs and a chaise-
longue with stuffing hanging out. A grate. MARWOOD
journeys into an adjoining room. Checks stairs and turns
back to a sink with a rusty pump. He drags the lever
down. A rheumatic whine. No water. The wind howls like
wolves. He moves back into the kitchen and discovers
WITHNAIL *sitting in a chair.*
MARWOOD: What are you doing?

A pair of shocked and horn-rimmed eyes focus in his direction.

WITHNAIL: Sitting down to enjoy my holiday.

Blasts of icy intensity rocket down the chimney. WITHNAIL could be standing on a cliff. MARWOOD checks out a huge range and turns back to WITHNAIL forcing the optimism.

MARWOOD: All right, we're gonna have to approach this scientifically. First thing is to get a fire alight. Then we'll split into two fact-finding groups. I'll deal with the water and other plumbings. You can check the fuel and wood situation.

41. INT. LIVING ROOM. COTTAGE. NIGHT.

With an abundance of acrid smoke a minute fire smoulders in the grate. MARWOOD dumps blankets and goes for the pump. Cranks violently. A dozen strokes and a flood of khaki water erupts. Euphoria. WITHNAIL barges through the front door in time to observe this phenomenon. Wet and gale-blasted and carrying a twig.

MARWOOD: What's that?

WITHNAIL: The fuel and wood situation. There's fuck all out there except a hurricane.

The fuel and wood situation gets thrown on the fire. One or two burnt-out logs in the grate. MARWOOD puts them on and joins WITHNAIL in the opposite chair. They stare into the fire. At every change of the wind they are engulfed in smoke.

This place is uninhabitable.

MARWOOD: Give it a chance. It's gotta warm up.

WITHNAIL: *Warm up?* We may as well sit round a cigarette.

MARWOOD *takes a large slug of whisky. Hands the bottle across.* WITHNAIL *practically finishes it. Lights a cigarette and starts coughing as he's temporarily obscured by another dose of smoke.*
This is ridiculous. We'll be found dead in here next spring. I've got a blinding, fucking headache. I must have heat.
So saying he rises to his pins and demolishes the nearest chair. Flames suddenly appear. WITHNAIL *assaults another and the room shifts through a speedy dissolve.*

42. INT. (ANOTHER ANGLE). LIVING ROOM. COTTAGE. NIGHT.
The room is filled with smoke. Only cigarette ends are visible. Both squat in their overcoats in front of a cold fire. WITHNAIL *slings another chair leg on.*
WITHNAIL: Whatever happens we've got to keep this bastard burning.
There's a door banging outside. The wind is devouring the house.
MARWOOD: We've got enough furniture for tonight. We'll get down that farm tomorrow and get logs.
WITHNAIL: All this is a mistake. I tell you. This is a dreadful mistake.

43. INT. BEDROOM. COTTAGE. DAY.
MARWOOD *wears his overcoat like a dressing gown. Boots like slippers. Wind still hammers the house. He looks out of his window. The rain has stopped. Little view except the side of a shed. Grabbing his clothes he shambles into* WITHNAIL's *room. Its occupant is heaped under blankets*

and overcoat and asleep. Decides not to wake him and quietly closes the door and heads downstairs.

44. INT. HALL/BOUDOIR. COTTAGE. DAY.
A tub full of walking sticks at the bottom of the stairs. Plus a hat rack featuring a couple of country-type caps and a fencing mask. MARWOOD notices an épée in the tub. He's about to walk out of the door when he decides to explore a room he missed last night . . . opens the door on to a Victorian-looking room. A 1930s record player with a stack of records. Dismal early Georgian furniture. Most of the chairs and paintings are decorated with dribbles of bird shit. He notices a dead (down the chimney) crow, before shutting the door and walking across the little outside yard.

45. EXT. COURTYARD. COTTAGE. DAY.
MARWOOD opens a wood-gate and walks down a short entrance of brick. Fumbles for his glasses and puts them on. And here it is! Here is a fifteen-mile-long picture postcard. Bleak but beautiful. A lake stretches away to the left furnished with pines. Optimism cuts in as he heads back to the house.

46. EXT. TRACK. HILLSIDE OVER FARM. DAY.
MARWOOD is fully dressed and filled with a slow puncture of enthusiasm. He carries a walking stick and wears a cheese-cutter cap. But the country image doesn't last long. It dissolves with every step. Midway between the cottage and the farmhouse his boots are saturated. Cows turn to see him pass. He comes to a halt at a gate. SHUT THIS GATE. A few yards past it and he sees why. Twenty feet in front of him is a big bull with horns on its head. Neither

of them likes the look of the other and MARWOOD *climbs a wall. No more path. This is virtually wading. At a safe distance he reclimbs the wall. Continues towards the farmhouse. The wind practically takes his glasses off. Angry black clouds massing.*

47. EXT. CROW CRAG FARMHOUSE. DAY.
A large and mysterious-looking building constructed of local stone. Curtains drawn and looks deserted.
MARWOOD *comes in over a fence and walks towards it. Clears the mud from his boots. An imposing front door. It takes a knockering. No response and another knock. Sounds of footsteps over stone.*
VOICE (O.S.): Who's there?
MARWOOD: Me.

> *The door opens. Here's an* OLD BIRD *in an apron and hobnailed boots.*

OLD BIRD: What do you want?

> MARWOOD *stares at her. She stares back. She's horrible and seventy and suspicious. Is this the crow that made the farm famous?*

MARWOOD: I'm a friend of Montague Withnail. He's lent us his cottage.

> *She freezes a hard so what?* MARWOOD *tries to smile at her. Fails.*

> I wondered if you could sell us some food? Eggs and things?

OLD CROW: No. We ain't a shop.
MARWOOD: What about wood and coal?
OLD CROW: No.

> *Maybe it's his accent she doesn't like. He tries another tack.*

50

MARWOOD: I'm not from London, you know.

HORRIBLE OLD CROW: I don't care where you come from.

And MARWOOD *gets a faceful of door. He stares at it a moment. Turns away. Walks fifteen feet backwards and looks at penned sheep. Looks at the house.*

MARWOOD (V.O.): Not the attitude I'd been given to expect from the H. E. Bates novel I'd read. I thought they'd all be out the back drinking cider and discussing butter. Clearly a myth.

He decides to have another go. Back to the door. Another knock. It starts to rain.

Evidently country people are no more receptive to strangers than city dwellers.

The footsteps return. But this time she declines to open up.

MARWOOD: D'you think you could tell me where I could buy some coal and wood?

OLD CROW (O.S.): You'll have to see my son. He runs this farm.

MARWOOD: Where is your son?

OLD CROW (O.S.): Up in top fields. You can't miss him. His leg's bound in polythene.

48. EXT. HILL OVER HOUSE/STREAM/COURTYARD. DAY.

MARWOOD *comes over the hill. Obviously slipped in shit more times than I care to detail. Angry and soaked to the skin, he pounds into the courtyard and disappears into the house.*

49. INT. KITCHEN. COTTAGE. DAY.

Rain beats the window. MARWOOD *beats the ceiling with a saucepan.*

MARWOOD: Wake up, you bastard. You have to get wood.
He works the pump. Washes himself with spurts of icy water. Finds time to continue bashing the ceiling with his pan.
Wake up! Wake up, you bastard!
A gale blows through the house. Without a fire the chimney is like having a hole in the roof. WITHNAIL *shuffles in wearing his overcoat. Catches a hostile glare as* MARWOOD *heads for the hearth and sits to wrench his boots off.*
WITHNAIL: Jesus – you're covered in shit.
MARWOOD: I tried to get fuel and wood. There's a miserable little pensioner down there. She wouldn't give it to me.
WITHNAIL: Where are we gonna get it then?
MARWOOD: There's a man up the mountain. Why he's up there, fuck knows. But he's up there with a leg bound in polythene. You can't miss him. He's the man.
MARWOOD *succeeds in removing his boots. Takes a slug of whisky.*
MARWOOD: Have another look in that shed. Find anything. And if you can't find anything, bring in the shed.

50. INT. LIVING ROOM. COTTAGE. DAY.
Another dining chair has gone on. The room is again filled with smoke. They sit on either side of the fire eating breakfast. Unsuitable foods under the circumstances. Plastic carrier bags produce an apple. A camembert. Whisky and wine. MARWOOD *cuts an apple in half and offers it to* WITHNAIL. *He refuses and lights a cigarette.*
MARWOOD: How come Monty owns such a horrible little shack?

52

WITHNAIL: I've no idea.

And he stands and starts pacing and the wind howls outside.

MARWOOD: Never discuss your family, do you?

WITHNAIL: I fail to see my family is of any interest to you – I have absolutely no interest in yours – I dislike relatives in general, and my own in particular.

MARWOOD: Why?

WITHNAIL *discovers an épée in the stick bin and fences the air.*

WITHNAIL: Because . . . I've told you why . . . we're incompatible. They don't like me being on stage.

MARWOOD: Then they must be delighted with your career.

WITHNAIL: What d'you mean?

MARWOOD: You rarely are.

MARWOOD's *cynicism inspires Shakespearian activity with the épée.*

WITHNAIL: You just wait. Just you wait. When I strike, they won't know what hit 'em.

A very low rumble a long way away. They hear it simultaneously and it takes WITHNAIL *to the door.* There's a tractor approaching.

MARWOOD *instantly animates. Begins shoving feet into his boots.*

MARWOOD: Get after him. That must be the man.

51. EXT. COTTAGE GARDENS/TRACK. DAY.

WITHNAIL *is attempting to cross a potato patch without damaging his boots. Bellowing* 'Get out of the way' MARWOOD *barges past. The wind takes their breath and voices away.* WITHNAIL *mounts the wall and stands on top of it, waving like a nancy sailor. This has zero affect*

*on the tractor. It's passing at speed about forty yards
away. Abandoning all regard for personal wellbeing*
MARWOOD *clambers the wall and races through the mud
waving his arms like a maniac. Finally manages to
attract the driver's attention. He stops and they descend
on him.*

*A face looks out of the cab. Registers alarm at the fury
of these idiots' approach.* WITHNAIL *grabs at a mudguard
as if to stop the tractor getting away. Shouts up at the
staring* FARMER.

WITHNAIL: Are you the farmer?

> *There is a reticence in* ISACS PARKIN *to speak with
> these two.*

MARWOOD: Shut up. I'll deal with this.

> MARWOOD *takes control and* ISACS PARKIN *shuts his
> engine down.*

WITHNAIL: We've gone on holiday by mistake. We're in
this cottage here.

> ISACS PARKIN *looks down at this shit-streaked wreck
> in surprise.*

Are you the farmer?

MARWOOD: Stop saying that, Withnail. Of course he's the
fucking farmer.

> *The farmer can't hear. Opens his door. A leg bound in
> polythene. Also a plaster cast. The polythene is
> evidently to keep out damp.*

We're friends of Montague Withnail. We desperately
need fuel and wood.

> *An exchange of eyes.* PARKIN *stares. Repeats*
> 'Montague Withnail?'

Montague Withnail. You must know him. He's a fat
man. He owns the cottage.

ISACS PARKIN: I seen a fat man. Lunnon type. Queer sort.
But his name's French or summit.

WITHNAIL: French?

ISACS PARKIN: Adrienne de la Touche. But he ain't been here
for a coupla years. Last time I seen him was with his son.
Even under these circumstances, MARWOOD *finds a
sort of a smile.*

MARWOOD: That's him.

WITHNAIL: Listen, we're bona fide. We don't come from
London. Can we have some fuel and wood?

ISACS PARKIN: I could bring you some logs up later. I
gotta feed the cows and that first.

WITHNAIL: When?

MARWOOD: Shut up. That would be very nice of you.
What about food? D'you think you could sell us
something to eat?

ISACS PARKIN: I could bring you a chicken. But you'll have
to go into the village really.

MARWOOD: That would be very kind of you.
PARKIN *swings his stiffened leg inside and starts the
engine.*
What happened to your leg?

ISACS PARKIN: Got a randy bull down there. Give us one
in the knee.
*He guns the engine and vanishes down the track.
Smiles emerge. They head back to the cottage with a
sense of achievement. It's going to get better. And Al
Bowley is already beginning to play.*

52. INT. LIVING ROOM. COTTAGE. DAY.
*A record continues to scrape. But things are looking up in
here. Logs are coming. And they have made free with the*

55

furniture. WITHNAIL's *almost whistling as he goes about his duties at the grate. He's invented some sort of draught deflector out of a sheet of iron. It is moderately successful in directing smoke up the chimney. He opens the oven door and shoves his boots in. Closes the door as* MARWOOD *appears from the kitchen. The latter removes a cauldron of boiling water from the fire.*

MARWOOD: You wanna get out the back, don't you? Get some spuds up?

WITHNAIL *doesn't like the idea. Has a perfect excuse.*
WITHNAIL: Sorry, I can't. My boots are in the oven.
MARWOOD: You'd go out if you had boots?
WITHNAIL: Gladly.

MARWOOD *stands and walks into the kitchen. Reappears instantly.* WITHNAIL *looks suspiciously at a pair of plastic carrier bags.*

MARWOOD: We can tie 'em up with string.

53. EXT. GARDEN. COTTAGE. DAY.
WITHNAIL *emerges from the front door wearing his overcoat and a pair of carrier bags. He clasps a carving fork and heads for the potato patch.* MARWOOD *stands at the door. Shouts directions concerning the location of the potato. The fork goes in and a fibrous little marble comes out.* 'I've got one. I've got one.'

54. EXT. COURTYARD. COTTAGE. NIGHT.
The camera stares in the window. WITHNAIL *asleep in front of the fire.* MARWOOD *at the table writing in his notebook in the light of an oil lamp. Several large peeled potatoes on the table. He looks up to think but gets interrupted by the sound of a tractor. Stands and heads for the door.*

The camera pulls back as the tractor rumbles in. The rain has stopped, but it's still blowing up rotten from the lake.

PARKIN *dumps logs and* MARWOOD *walks round to his cab. He smiles up at the farmer offering thanks and how much do I owe?*

ISACS PARKIN: You can pay us when you come down.

MARWOOD: What about the chicken?

ISACS PARKIN: He's on the back. In the sack.

55. INT. LIVING ROOM. COTTAGE. EVENING.

MARWOOD *shakes* WITHNAIL *into consciousness. Directs his attention towards a sack on the floor.*

MARWOOD: Parkin's been. There's the supper.

> *The bag starts to move. Without getting into the mechanics a chicken finds a way out.*

WITHNAIL: What are we supposed to do with that?

MARWOOD: Eat it.

WITHNAIL: Eat it. The fucker's alive.

MARWOOD: I know that. You've gotta kill it.

WITHNAIL: Me? I'm the fire lighter and fuel collector.

MARWOOD: I know that. But I got the logs in.

> *The chicken starts to walk.*

WITHNAIL: Follow it.

MARWOOD: It takes away your appetite looking at it.

WITHNAIL: No it doesn't, I'm starving. How can we make it die?

MARWOOD: You have to throttle them.

> *Suddenly it leaps in the air and momentarily drives them off.*

I think you should strangle it instantly, in case it starts trying to make friends with us.

WITHNAIL: All right, get hold of it. You hold it down, and I'll strangle it.

MARWOOD: I couldn't. It's got dreadful beady eyes. It's staring me out.

WITHNAIL: It's a *fucking chicken*. Just think of it with bacon across its back.

WITHNAIL's volume propels the chicken into the kitchen. He follows it, pausing at the kitchen door.

All right, I'll deal with this, but you'll have to get its guts out.

56. INT. KITCHEN. COTTAGE. NIGHT.

Firelight in the living room and candlelight in here.
MARWOOD has finished preparations. A muzzle of a shotgun prods at the back of his head. He turns and knocks the double barrel aside.

MARWOOD: Never point guns at people. It' extremely dangerous. Where'd you get it?

WITHNAIL: Cupboard.

MARWOOD: Well put it back. What about this roasting dish?

WITHNAIL shakes his head and turns on the chicken with his gun. The barrels poke at it. It's still in possession of its feet and a considerable amount of feathers.

MARWOOD: What are we gonna cook it in?

WITHNAIL: You're the food and plumbings man. I've no idea. I wish I'd found this an hour ago. I'd have taken great pleasure in gunning this pullet down.

The gun is lowered and WITHNAIL applies himself to the chicken.

WITHNAIL: Shouldn't it be more bald than that?

MARWOOD: No, it shouldn't. All right, we're gonna have to reverse the roles. We'll bake the potatoes in the oven, and boil this bastard over the fire.

A large iron kettle. They attempt to stuff it in. Head first. Won't go. MARWOOD *reverses it. Arse next. Won't go.* WITHNAIL *punches it. But this pullet is not going to go in this kettle.*

WITHNAIL: Let's get its feet off.

MARWOOD *shakes his head and walks purposefully towards the oven.*

MARWOOD: No, it's gonna need its feet.

He opens the oven door. Instructs WITHNAIL *to remove his boots. They come out steaming on the end of a poker.*

MARWOOD *replaces them with a brick. Positioned side on at the bottom of the oven.*

It can stand with its legs either side of that.

MARWOOD *mounts it upright looking out towards the door.* WITHNAIL *bastes his hands as another door is slammed in the chicken's face.*

57. EXT. COUNTRYSIDE. DAY.

About as much countryside as a Super Panavision lens is capable of handling. The lake and the sky and the mountains look anaemic. This is a huge panorama. Somewhere in the middle of it is a tiny telephone booth.

WITHNAIL (V.O.): I've already put two shillings in. No. I haven't got another. It's not my fault if the system doesn't work.

58. EXT. TELEPHONE BOOTH. COUNTRY ROAD/LAKESIDE.
DAY.

WITHNAIL *shoves his head out. Like* MARWOOD *several days' beard.*

WITHNAIL: The bitch hung up on me.

> *A search for more change begins.* WITHNAIL *has none and* MARWOOD *a single two shilling piece. Reluctantly offers it to* WITHNAIL.

MARWOOD: I'll phone tomorrow. I don't wanna call anyway.

> MARWOOD *squeezes into the booth to escape the icy wind. Redialling takes effect and* WITHNAIL *is connected surprisingly quickly.*

Don't wanna hear I haven't got it.

> *A combination of bad line and emotion causes* WITHNAIL *to shout.*

WITHNAIL: Hello? How are you? Very well. A what? Why wouldn't they see me? . . . This is ridiculous, I haven't been for a job for three months. Understudy Constantine? I'm not gonna understudy Constantine. Why can't I play the part? That's ridiculous. No I'm not in London. Penrith. *Penrith.* Well what about TV? Listen, I pay you ten per cent to do that. What? Well lick ten per cent of the asses for me then. Hello? Hello? Hello? How dare you. Fuck you.

> *He bashes the receiver down and follows* MARWOOD *out of the box.*

Bastard asked me to understudy Constantine in *The Seagull.*

> *They start walking up the road.* MARWOOD *clutching a grocery bag.*

I'm not gonna understudy anybody. Specially that little

pimp. Anyway, I loathe those Russian plays. Always full of women staring out of windows, whining about ducks going to Moscow.

59. EXT. TRACK. MOUNTAINSIDE. DAY.
Sodden fields. The mountains seem to have an inexhaustible supply of liquids. The reality of agents has depressed them both. They proceed carefully to avoid puncturing bags.

WITHNAIL: What d'you think of Desmond Wolfe?

MARWOOD: In respect of what?

WITHNAIL: I'm thinking of changing my name.

MARWOOD: It's too like Donald Wolfit . . .

Pausing for breath, MARWOOD *stops. Thrusts the groceries across.*

Change-over point . . .

WITHNAIL *looks up at the tractor descending from the top fields.*

WITHNAIL: D'you think he's happier than us?

MARWOOD: No.

He opens the gate and WITHNAIL *follows through. They continue walking. Absorbed in their own thoughts. The tractor is about a hundred yards away. It stops suddenly and* ISACS PARKIN *sticks his head out. For some reason he waves frantically and they wave back.*

WITHNAIL: I suppose happiness is relative . . .

ISACS PARKIN *is back in his tractor. Gunning the engine and racing towards them in a haze of mud. And still waving frantically.*

. . . but I never thought it would be a polythene bag without a hole in it.

MARWOOD *isn't listening. Watches* ISACS PARKIN
drive like a maniac.

MARWOOD: What's the matter with him?

MARWOOD *suddenly swings round. Wide eyed. The
question is answered.*

MARWOOD: You didn't shut the gate.

*The farmer is driving dangerously. Head stuck out and
screaming.*

ISACS PARKIN: Shut that gate. Shut that gate.

*But it's too late. They stand paralysed in their bags.
Watch as the bull charges up the field and crashes
through the opening.*

Stop that bull. Stop that bull.

Thrusting the groceries across WITHNAIL *runs for it
and literally dives over the nearest wall.* ISACS
PARKIN *leaps from his tractor and poles across the
field like Long John Silver.* 'Stop that bull. Stop that
bull.' *Five yards separation and the bull stops.*
MARWOOD *freezes.* WITHNAIL's *head comes back
over the wall.*

WITHNAIL: Grab its ring.

MARWOOD *holds the groceries out in front of him as
though offering some sort of sacrifice. A flimsy barrier
between himself and four thousand pounds of angry
hamburger waiting to take revenge.*

Keep your bag up. Out vibe it.

With a terrified sneer MARWOOD *stares into its
bloodshot eyes. Breath like a Ferrari revving up.
Exhaust from either nostril.*

It wants to get up there and fuck those cows.

ISACS PARKIN *arrives but can't get over the wall
because of his stiffened leg.* MARWOOD *is the pig in*

the middle. WITHNAIL *looking over the wall the farmer looking over the wall opposite.*

ISACS PARKIN: Show no fear.

The bull starts hoof actions in the mud. MARWOOD *stares in terror. This is quite possibly an advertisement preceding the charge.*

Show no fear. Just run at it.

MARWOOD: That can't be sensible, can it? The bastard's about to run at me.

ISACS PARKIN: He's randy.

MARWOOD: Yes, yes, I know he is.

WITHNAIL: He wants to have sex with those cows.

MARWOOD: Shut up Withnail.

ISACS PARKIN: Run at it shouting.

WITHNAIL: Do as he says. Start shouting.

Seems like the shouting is imminent anyway. Also the running. The only concern troubling MARWOOD *is the direction the running is advised. On the edge of vision he sees* WITHNAIL *light a cigarette!*

WITHNAIL: It won't gore you.

MARWOOD's *voice sounds like Richard III at some sort of climax.*

MARWOOD: A coward, you are, Withnail. An expert on bulls, you are not.

This statement is delivered with considerable emotion. Violence towards WITHNAIL *drives* MARWOOD *towards the bull. Vegetables fly as he descends in his carrier bags shouting at the top of his voice. The bull is astonished by what's coming at him. Apparently even less prepared to get charged than charge himself. He turns instantly and hot hoofs it back through the opening.* PARKIN *hobbles at speed and closes the gate*

*behind him. As soon as he's convinced the danger is
over* WITHNAIL *clambers back over the wall.*

   MARWOOD *is trembling and in a state of shock.
He picks up stray vegetables from the mud.* PARKIN
shouts 'Keep this gate shut.' *And legs off as though
he has just finished the shit/crop allocation in time
for tea.*

WITHNAIL: I think an evening at the Crow.

   MARWOOD *grabs a turnip. The experience has frozen
his senses.*

MARWOOD: An evening at the Crow? I could have been
   killed.

WITHNAIL: Nahh. Parkin knew what he was doing.

MARWOOD: Sure he did. An absolute fucking authority.
   That's why he couldn't get over the wall.

WITHNAIL: Don't wanna overdo it, do you?

   *Both daylight and the image are dissolving as they
   head up the hill.*

WITHNAIL: We're in the countryside. Things like this are
   perfectly normal.

60. INT. LIVING ROOM. COTTAGE. EVENING.
The dissolve completes into candlelight and firelight.
MARWOOD *sits in front of the latter writing in his
notebook with the assistance of the former. Big shadows
on the wall behind him.* WITHNAIL *is fencing with himself
again. Got a cigarette stuck in his maw. Decides to involve*
MARWOOD *in the exercise and starts prodding selected
areas of his back and neck.* MARWOOD *swats him off like
an unwelcome wasp. But the wasp comes back.*
WITHNAIL: C'mon . . . on your pins.
MARWOOD: Stop it. I'm thinking.

The poing of the épée pokes the very centre of
MARWOOD's *head.*

WITHNAIL: C'mon. 'Here's my fiddlestick; here's that shall make you dance!'
And he prods and pokes further selected areas of MARWOOD's *body. With increasing annoyance the recipient knocks the épée away.* WITHNAIL *removes his cigarette to intone à la Shakespeare.*

WITHNAIL: Oh calm, dishonourable, vile submission! Come on, you rat-catcher, will you walk?

MARWOOD: Last time I fought you, I thrashed you into the ground.

WITHNAIL: Thou speakest bollocks. C'mon.
MARWOOD *is suddenly on his feet, retrieves another épée from the walking-stick tub. Now he's facing* WITHNAIL *across the table.*

MARWOOD: All right, Withnail. Prepare to die. Three hits to win, loser buys the drinks.
Here comes some Errol Flynn – and if it's spelt wrong it's because it's fought wrong. But these boys can fence – evidently part of their drama school training. I'm not going to describe it because I don't know what it'll look like till we're there. But MARWOOD *gets a poke, 'One' into* WITHNAIL's *throttle, which enrages him. Fag still burning he lunges at the coat hooks and grabs the mask. 'Right, you bastard', and the mask goes on.*
The fight continues. WITHNAIL *has donned the mask with his cigarette still in his mouth – a thing like a smoking beehive is slashing around the premises.* MARWOOD *finally wins.* WITHNAIL *takes 'Three' and is down on the table point in his neck –* 'Yield? Yield?' *And he does yield.*

61. EXT. COUNTRY ROAD. NIGHT.

WITHNAIL *and* MARWOOD *pound along in the moonlight.*
A spiteful wind coming off the lake. Also reflections of a
tiny village. Their destination is one of the few buildings
emitting light.

MARWOOD (V.O.): If the Crow and Cunt ever had life it
was dead now. It was like walking into a lung. A
sulphur-stained nicotine-yellow and fly-blown lung. Its
landlord was a retired alcoholic with military
pretensions and a complexion like the inside of a tea
pot.

62. INT. CROW AND CUNT. PUBLIC HOUSE. NIGHT.

A pair of small rooms with a log fire at one end and a
bar in the middle. Thick smoke and packed with men,
mainly wankers from the local farms. One or two
shepherds. Everything is yellow except for the landlord
who is bright red. Years of consistent boozing have gone
into this face. It also has a large moustache. WITHNAIL
and MARWOOD *squat on stools at the bar in front of*
him.

MARWOOD (V.O.): By the time the doors opened he was
arse-holed on rum, and got progressively more arse-
holed till he could take no more and fell over about
twelve o'clock.

WITHNAIL: We'll have another pair of large Scotches.
They watch in fascination as the GENERAL *lunges for*
his bottles. He hands them the drinks and turns to his
till to ring up. The money drawer shoots out. Catches
him in the gut and he staggers. Ricocheting off the bar
he throws himself on the till. Grabs a fistful of change
and slaps it on the counter.

THE GENERAL: I thought I was going for a minute . . .

His voice is circa 1942 with faint undertones of
Mancunian.

But no man has ever put me down. Have you had
training in the martial arts?

WITHNAIL: Yes, as a matter of fact I have. Before I
became a journalist, I was in the Territorials.

THE GENERAL *attempts to focus on* WITHNAIL *with*
his sepia eyes.

THE GENERAL: D'you know, when you first came in here,
I knew you'd been a services man. You can never
disguise it.

A cigarette is offered and WITHNAIL *lights up like Jack*
the Lad.

WITHNAIL: What were you in?

THE GENERAL: Tanks. North Africa Corps. A little before
your time. Don't spose you've engaged, have you?

WITHNAIL: Ireland . . .

THE GENERAL: Ah, a crack at the Mick.

WITHNAIL: Exactly. We'll have a couple more.

THE GENERAL: These shall be my pleasure.

He swings their glasses under the bottle and
repositions them.

What are you doing up here, then?

WITHNAIL: Feature for *Country Life.* We're doing a survey
of rural types. You know, farmers, travelling tinkers,
milkmen, that sort of thing.

Steadying himself on the bar the GENERAL *leans in on*
WITHNAIL *as though trying to get the end of his*
moustache into his ear.

THE GENERAL: Have you met Jake?

WITHNAIL *shakes his head and backs away from a*

*disturbing exhalation from the landlord's gut. His tone
is almost conspiratorial.*

Poacher. Works the lake. But keep it under your hat.
With what is virtually a salute WITHNAIL *acknowledges
this confidence and they make their way to corner
seats near the fire.*

The image is soft focus and sideways. It is from the
GENERAL's *point of view. As he straightens up it
straightens up. Focus improves and he looks across his
now nearly empty establishment, calling* 'Time,
Gentlemen.'

*All the shepherds and wankers have gone home. The
fire has gone out. Only* WITHNAIL *and* MARWOOD *in
front of its embers.* WITHNAIL *looks across. The*
GENERAL *is supporting himself on the beer pumps like
a man on crutches. His jaw is firmly clenched.*

MARWOOD: I think he means it.

*The time has approached when they're all too pissed
to know what time it is.* WITHNAIL *finishes his drink
and they stand to leave.*

*The door swings open and an alarming-looking
creature walks in. Around his neck are a dozen mole
traps linked to a length of sisal rope that disappears
into his hunchback. Loops of string are tied under his
knees. Above them a pair of massive bulges like
deformed thigh muscles. This is obviously* JAKE *the
poacher.*

*They watch as he heads for the bar. Pulls his own
pint and downs it as quickly as a pint can be poured
from a glass. A formidable sight. Like a tree has
uprooted itself and come in because it fancied a drink.
But respect from the* GENERAL. *He gets himself*

upright to pull the next pint. These drinks are
evidently free. A detail that doesn't go unnoticed.
WITHNAIL *leads the way across.*

  A pair of Scotches are ordered. And delivered. And
on the house. JAKE's *clothes are a mixture of earth*
and tweed and blood and decaying vegetables. A stink
comes off them buckling MARWOOD's *nostrils.* JAKE
is half-way through his pint when his bulges move. It
causes him discomfort. Plunging a hand under his belt
he extracts a pair of half-dead eels. They take a
terrible bashing on the counter and return to the
interior of his trouser. A pair of astonished faces
stare. MARWOOD *leans into* WITHNAIL *with a*
whisper.

MARWOOD: Ask him if we can have one.
WITHNAIL: What for?
MARWOOD: So we can eat it. We're fed up with stew.
  WITHNAIL *moves in and addresses* JAKE *as though he*
  were a waiter.
WITHNAIL: Excuse me. Could we have an eel?
  The tree turns towards him. Doesn't like the look of
  this prat.
  You've got eels down your leg.
JAKE: You leave them alone. Ain't nothin' down their
  interest to you.
  Ignoring WITHNAIL *he returns to his elbows and beer.*
  Finishing his pint and suddenly tugs at the rope
  vanishing into his hump.
  Help I, Raymond Goff. These be fed from ass-'ole to
  beak.
  The GENERAL *grabs at the rope. With difficulty he*
  pulls a brace of pheasant over JAKE's *head and*

conceals them behind the bar. More astonishment from MARWOOD *and* WITHNAIL. *And more whispers.*

The poacher gestures towards the whisky. Everyone gets a glass.

MARWOOD: What about one of these pheasants?

WITHNAIL *is reluctant.* JAKE *is preparing to leave. Now or never.*

Go on. Ask him.

The GENERAL *collapses on a stack of beer crates.* JAKE *rattles his traps and ties his coat with the rope.* WITHNAIL *works a smile.*

WITHNAIL: Excuse me. We were wondering whether we could purchase a pheasant off of you?

JAKE: No . . . I ain't got nothin' to sell.

WITHNAIL: Come on, old boy. What's in your hump?

JAKE *puts his face into* WITHNAIL. *Skin like the sole of a foot.*

JAKE: Now look you here. Them pheasants there are fer his pot. These eels is fer my pot. What makes you think I should give ya summat fer yer pot?

WITHNAIL: What pot?

MARWOOD: Our cooking pot.

JAKE: Arr, he knows. Give I wheeze on that fag.

MARWOOD *hands the cigarette across.* JAKE *sucks a deep inhalation. He hands it back and* MARWOOD *ashtrays it for fear of contamination. A Gauloise is offered.* JAKE *takes three. Wraps them in his hanky.*

I might see you lads in the week. I might put a rabbit your way.

MARWOOD: We don't want a rabbit. We want a pheasant.

JAKE: Now look you here ya young prat, I ain't got no pheasants. I aint' got no birds, no more an' you do.

70

WITHNAIL: Of course you have. You're the poacher.

Not a very sensitive remark. JAKE *is clearly upset by this accusation. Exploring his trousers he withdraws one of his eels.*

JAKE: If I hear more wordsa you. I'll put one of these here black pods on yer.

The eel wraps itself up Jake's arm. A rapid retreat as he menaces the creature in WITHNAIL's *face.*

WITHNAIL: Don't threaten me with a dead fish.

JAKE: Half-dead he might be. But I'll come on up after ye, and wake you up with a live one.

WITHNAIL: Sod your pheasants. You'll have to find us first.

WITHNAIL's *indignation has propelled him to the door. As* MARWOOD *follows him through* JAKE *raises his voice to bid them farewell.*

JAKE: Oh, I know where you are. You two's up at Crow Crag. I been watchin' you. Especially you, prancin' like a tit.

63. EXT. MOUNTAIN TRACK. OVER LAKE. NIGHT.

Several superior brains have dealt with nights like this. Here are raging moons and starry-starry nights.

MARWOOD *and* WITHNAIL *labour through the mire. The latter breathless and staggering.*

WITHNAIL: If I see that silage heap hanging around up here, I'll take the bastard axe to him.

The cottage comes into sight. Indigo slates in the moonlight. WITHNAIL *staggers to a wall and shouts at five miles of lake.*

Bastards. Bastards. Bastards.

Nobody to reply except an echo. As loud and as drunk as he is.

71

You'll all suffer. (Suffer. Suffer. Suffer.) I'll show the lot of you. (You. You. You.) I'm gonna be a star. (Star. Star. Star. Star. Star.)

He turns away and the echo fades into the black and starry night.

64. INT. LIVING ROOM. COTTAGE. DAY.

A load of weather on the roof. A large fire in the grate.
MARWOOD *is stirring in the kettle. Fishes something out. Tastes it and decides it's ready.*WITHNAIL *is at the dining table. Already hacked one crust off and is working at the opposite end of the loaf. A complaint from* MARWOOD *as he transfers kettle to table.*

MARWOOD: What are you doing?

WITHNAIL: Getting the crusts. I like the crusts.

MARWOOD: So do I. You can have that one. The other one's mine when we get to it.

    MARWOOD *sits and* WITHNAIL *peers into the kettle.*

WITHNAIL: Vegetables again? We'll sprout fucking feelers soon. Must be twenty thousand sheep out there on those fucking volcanoes, and we got a plateful of carrots.

MARWOOD: There's black puddings in it.

WITHNAIL: Black puddings are no good to us.

    He suddenly pushes his plate aside and rises to his feet.

I want something's flesh!

65. MOUNTAINSIDE. MOUNTAIN STREAM. DAY.

The water is freezing and fast running and so is WITHNAIL. *With bare feet and trousers rolled up above his knees he charges up the centre of the stream loosing off his shotgun.*

Massive explosions of water. A single fish is atomised.
MARWOOD *stands in his bags on the bank watching. Sees*
another fish. Directs WITHNAIL *who fires. Empty gun. He*
reloads. Fires. The fish has gone.

66. EXT. HILLSIDE TRACK. DAY.
Late afternoon. They walk fishless through the fields. Both
are bagless. Both dejected. Even the sheep look pissed off.
WITHNAIL: I think I'll call myself Donald Twain.

> *They turn off the track and head down the hillside*
> *towards the cottage. About twenty yards above it*
> *when* WITHNAIL *commands 'Stop.' With knees bent he*
> *goes into a sort of running crouch to a wall.*
>
> MARWOOD *follows. 'Keep down. He'll see you.'*
> *They both peer over the wall. A dark bundle of*
> *overcoat and savage hair is squinting into the living*
> *room window of the cottage. Hard to identify at first.*
> *Then no mistaking it. To* WITHNAIL's *horror it is*
> JAKE, *armed with a shotgun.*

WITHNAIL: It's him. What does he want?
MARWOOD: Better get down there and ask him.

> *He attempts to stand.* MARWOOD *pulls him down.*
> *Fear in the larynx.*

WITHNAIL: Don't be a fool! He's got a gun. The bastards's
psychotic, you've only gotta look at him.

> JAKE *is evidently tired of his investigations and is*
> *heading back towards the lake. He stops and turns for*
> *a last look and they cautiously climb the wall with*
> WITHNAIL *muttering about precautions.*

67. INT. LIVING ROOM. (KITCHEN). COTTAGE. NIGHT.
MARWOOD *is in front of the fire reading a play* Journey's

End *by R. C. Sherriff.* WITHNAIL *has produced a huge rusty bolt from somewhere and nails it to the kitchen door. Security is completed with a shovel rammed under the door knob. He then loads the shotgun and returns to the living room.*

WITHNAIL: This place has become impossible.

A sinister wind slams night doors. MARWOOD *ignores the diatribe.*

Freezing cold . . . perpetual rain . . . and now a fucking madman on the prowl outside, with eels.

MARWOOD: All right, you've made your point. We'll pack up and get out tomorrow.

Their boots stand in the grate and socks stand next to them. MARWOOD *tests one of his. Baked stiff. Starts putting it on.*

WITHNAIL: What are you doing?

MARWOOD: Going for a slash.

WITHNAIL: No you're not. You can't. I can't get my boots on when they're hot.

MARWOOD: I'll go alone.

WITHNAIL *doesn't like the sound of this and rockets to his feet.*

WITHNAIL: No you won't. You're not leaving me in here alone. Those are the kind of windows faces look in at.

68. INT. STAIRWAY. COTTAGE. NIGHT.

Owls and wind and doors banging. Candlelight on the stairs.

WITHNAIL: In both our interests I think we should sleep together.

MARWOOD: Don't be ridiculous. He's not coming up here in the dark.

MARWOOD *opens a window at the top of the stairs and takes a piss.*

WITHNAIL: Of course he is. He's on that lake every night. And if he decides to come up here and catches one of us unawares, he's got a much better chance of dealing with the other.

MARWOOD: No.

He closes the window followed by his bedroom door on WITHNAIL.

69. INT. BEDROOM. COTTAGE. NIGHT.

MARWOOD *is obviously in the middle of a pleasant dream. Occasionally chuckling in his sleep. The door opens and a candle comes in followed by* WITHNAIL *and shotgun.*
MARWOOD *starts back as he wakes. Blinks at this spectrelike figure in Y-fronts.*

WITHNAIL: What's the matter with you?

MARWOOD *is too drowsy to answer.* WITHNAIL *is drenched in terror.*

What are you laughing at?

MARWOOD: I was dreaming. What d'you want?

WITHNAIL: You frightened the piss out of me. Move over. I'm getting in.

MARWOOD *resists but a pocked legs forces itself under the covers. A brief struggle follows.* WITHNAIL *manages to get into the bed.*

Huge shadows in the candlelight. A dispute over the blankets. It resolves itself with MARWOOD'S *arse thrust in the icy air.*

MARWOOD: This is ridiculous. I'll have to sleep in your bed.

WITHNAIL: I'll have to come with you then.

MARWOOD: Will you get out?

WITHNAIL: No.

MARWOOD: Then I will.

They both get out together. Stare at each other. Both get back in together. MARWOOD *is prepared to tolerate* WITHNAIL *but not his shotgun. It's positioned across the bed below their chins.*

All right. You can stay. But the gun doesn't.

WITHNAIL: I must keep the gun. I intend to remain awake till morning.

MARWOOD *snaps up in the bed. Attempts to confiscate the shotgun.*

MARWOOD: This is my bed, and I demand precedence in it. Give me the gun.

WITHNAIL: No.

A fight in the bed begins. Little to see but two heads and a muzzle and a heap of writhing blankets. The gun goes off. Blows a fucking great hole in the wall behind the bed. A paralysis. Silence. Smoke and dust settle. Then MARWOOD *emerges with an explosion as violent as the gun.* 'You mad fucking bastard.' *He storms across the room and launches the weapon head first through the window. A shattering of glass. Then this terrific door slam as he pounds out to sleep in* WITHNAIL's *room.*

70. INT. BEDROOM. COTTAGE. NIGHT.

A door banging as wind blunders to the lake. Owls hooting in the distance. MARWOOD *is asleep. The door opens. The candle comes in followed by* WITHNAIL. *Face ruptured with terror. The candle goes down on the bedside table and a hand clamps over* MARWOOD's *mouth.*

76

MARWOOD *wakes choking for breath and the hand gets bashed aside.* WITHNAIL *dances around. Finger over lips. A gesture for silence.*

MARWOOD: Get out. Fuck you. Fuck off.

With hands waving like a hypnotist WITHNAIL *screams in a whisper.*

WITHNAIL: Shut up. Listen. Listen.

MARWOOD *tries to focus his ears and eyes but manages only temper.*

MARWOOD: There's nothing. Get to bed.

He hunches back under the blankets. WITHNAIL *decides to join him.*

WITHNAIL: I heard a noise. I must get in.

MARWOOD: Oh, for fuck's sake.

WITHNAIL *gets into the bed.* MARWOOD *turns over. There is a noise.*

What was that?

WITHNAIL: That's it. That's it.

MARWOOD: What is it?

WITHNAIL: It's the maniac.

MARWOOD *sits up. Myopic ears straining at the darkness. The door continues to bang. But nothing suspicious and the noise has gone.*

MARWOOD: Probably foxes looking for grub.

WITHNAIL *suddenly stiffens in the bed. Knocks the candle over which extinguishes as it hits the floor. Faint moonlight now illuminates the room.*

WITHNAIL: Listen. Listen.

No mistaking it this time. Definitely a suspicious movement outside. Here come the wide eyes and sweat. Both are now bolt upright in the bed. Hearts revving up as the adrenalin squirts in. Sound re-invades the silence.

Unmistakably the grind of gravel under the heel of a heavy boot. An exchange of tiny whispers.

MARWOOD: Maybe it's the farmer.

WITHNAIL: At two o'clock in the morning? It's the killer. He's come to kill us. What are we gonna do?

The feet are heading round the house towards the kitchen door. A rattle and a banging as the intruder shakes the securities.

He wants to come in. He's trying to get in.

MARWOOD: Be quiet. He can't. He'll go away.

They follow the footsteps with their ears. After several indecisive tramplings they get fainter and move away from the house.

MARWOOD: He's going . . .

WITHNAIL has gone up six octaves. Like a whispering choir boy.

WITHNAIL: This is all your fault. You've even given him the fucking gun.

For a few moments a silence that promises perpetuality. Then both are shattered with the glass of the living room window.

He's coming through the fucking window. He's getting in.

An aggressive grunt downstairs as the intruder attempts to force his way in. WITHNAIL *is stiff as a board and practically levitating. Though* MARWOOD *is equally terrified, he plans some sort of defence. Grabs the candle.* 'Gimme the matches.' *A Walt Disney mouse replies.* 'Downstairs.' *And so is Jake. They hear his feet make contact with the stone floor. Then again profound silence.* WITHNAIL *vices a hand on to* MARWOOD. *Gurgles* 'He's in.' *And then shoves the*

78

sheet in his mouth. They stare into the boulders of silence. Then a hair-raising panic-striking sound. WITHNAIL *gags through the sheet.* 'He's sharpening a fucking knife.'

MARWOOD: We'll have to tackle him. You stay in bed and pretend to be asleep. He'll go for you. When he does I'll leap on his back.

MARWOOD attempts to implement his plan but WITHNAIL detains him.

WITHNAIL: No. No. It'll be too late. I'll be knifed by then. We'll have to try and make friends with him.

The latch clicks on the door at the bottom of the stairs. Then a creak of wood as footsteps mount. Slow heavy treads of unfamiliarity with the house. A pause. They head for MARWOOD's room.

Although WITHNAIL is atrophied with fear he pushes at MARWOOD's back with marshmallow arms. Interprets Jake's direction as a signal of his intentions.

WITHNAIL: He's gone into your room. It's you he wants. Offer him yourself.

A terrible moment of silence. Then the feet head back. The bed is thrashing the wall in record of their heart beats. The door knob turns. A yellow beam of torch light. A low sustained rattle escapes WITHNAIL's throat. Like a death rattle. The cry of a coward in crisis. Perhaps he's just died of a heart attack.

Heads press back into the pillows. The beam dazzles their eyes. A voice tangled with saliva and griding teeth attempts speech. Several breathless grunts before he falls back in the pillow.

WITHNAIL: We mean no harm . . .

*The beam lowers itself. A chuckle. A towering figure.
It speaks.*

MONTY: Dear boys. Dear boys. Forgive me.
*Total silence. Followed by total relief. Followed by
total anger.*

MARWOOD: Monty. Monty. Monty.

WITHNAIL: Monty. You terrible cunt!

MONTY: Forgive me. It was inconsiderate of me not to
have telegrammed.

WITHNAIL: What are you doing? Prowling around in the
middle of the fucking night?
*WITHNAIL's bark redirects his uncle's torch. He coyly
examines the floorboards. Clearly he thinks he's
disturbed them at it.*

MONTY: I had a punctured tyre. I had to wait an aeon
for assistance. I'm sorry if I disturbed you. I should
have knocked. I'll sleep in the spare room tonight if
I may.

MARWOOD: Anywhere you like.

71. LIVING ROOM. COTTAGE. DAY.
*Sounds of chopping outside. Squares of sunshine on the
wall. An unusual sight. The first clear day. Apart from
socks and boots MARWOOD walks in fully dressed. An
almost remarkable transformation. He scans the changes as
he applies his boots. Floor swept and fire blazing. A huge
bowl of fruit on the table. No broken windows. Monty
has worked magic in here. Elbowing his coat MARWOOD
walks into the kitchen.*

*Work surfaces scrubbed. Floor mopped. A stack of
exclusive groceries on the table. And under it a cardboard
box containing several joints of meat. Monty clearly*

intends to stay for a while. And here he is. Plus fours.
Hiking boots. And an armful of logs.

MONTY: Good morning. Did you sleep well?

> MARWOOD *follows him into the living room.* MONTY
> *dumps the wood.*

> I do apologise for last night. It was perfectly
> inconsiderate of me.

MARWOOD: Perfectly all right, Monty. You've been busy
in here?

JAKE: As a bee.

> *He cavorts back into the kitchen. And unwraps a deck*
> *of bacon.*

MARWOOD: How did you repair the window?

MONTY: I didn't break it. Merely forced it a little. Sorry if
I frightened you, there was an empty wine bottle on
the ledge.

> MONTY *prods rashers with a fork. An exercise he*
> *doesn't enjoy.*

> Why don't you go and wake him? Breakfast in fifteen
> minutes.

72. INT. LIVING ROOM. COTTAGE. DAY.

The improvements in living standards haven't gone
unnoticed by WITHNAIL. *Breakfast has matured into*
Turkish cigarettes. MONTY *beams with pleasure.*

> *An appropriate moment for a rendition of Alfred, Lord*
> *Tennyson.*

MONTY: The old order changeth, yielding place to new. And
God fulfils himself in many ways. And soon, I suppose, I
shall be swept away by some vulgar little tumor.

> *The moment mists his eyes. His head shakes. His voice*
> *vaporises.*

Ah, my boys, my boys, we're at the end of an age. We live in a land of weather forecasts, and breakfasts that 'set in'. Shat on by Tories. Shovelled up by Labour. And here we are. We three. Perhaps the last island of beauty in the world.

He takes their hands. For a moment it seems he's going to shove them in his mouth. An exchange of eyes. And then MONTY *smiles.*

Now which one of you is going to be a splendid fellow and go down to the Rolls for the rest of the things?

MARWOOD *and* WITHNAIL *stand simultaneously and speak simultaneously.*

MARWOOD/WITHNAIL: I will.

MARWOOD: No, I'd better go. I've got to see about digging the car out, anyway.

MONTY: We have my car, dear boy.

MARWOOD: Yes, but if it rains, we're buggered.

Or words to that effect. MONTY *doesn't notice.* MARWOOD *stutters.*

MARWOOD: I mean . . . we'll never get it out . . .

A surprising enthusiasm from WITHNAIL *as he reaches for his bags.*

WITHNAIL: We'll deal with the car when I get back. Leave this to me.

MARWOOD: I'll come with you then. I fancy a walk.

MONTY: No, no. I'm told you're a little wizard in the kitchen. I'll need you to work on the joint.

WITHNAIL: Yeah. You're the cook.

MONTY raises an eyebrow as WITHNAIL *begins shaking out his footwear.*

We forgot to bring Wellingtons . . .

MONTY: But how dreadful. You mean you've been up here

in all this beastly mud and oomska without
Wellingtons?
WITHNAIL *nods and heads for the kitchen door.*
MONTY *follows. And somewhat peeved* MARWOOD
paces after them. WITHNAIL *tramps outside and*
MARWOOD *sees them both through the kitchen
window.*
This afternoon I'm going to take you both into
Penrith, and get you fitted with some good-quality
rubber boots.

73. INT. KITCHEN. COTTAGE. DAY.
MARWOOD *seems worried to be alone with the uncle.
They're both midway through unpacking the supplies. A
bombardment of smiles from* MONTY *every time their eyes
meet.* MARWOOD *does his best to return them. But nerves
force lips into a sort of sneer.* MONTY *uses a napkin to
remove a massive leg of lamb from his box. He shoves it
at* MARWOOD *who holds it like a father with his newly
born baby.* MONTY *chirps towards another box.*
MONTY: Garlic, rosemary and salt.
   *He plunges into a grocery sack. A tablecloth and
   napkins and a pair of aprons. Slips into one. Goes for*
   MARWOOD *with the other.*
MONTY: I brought two in case either of you was any good
   in the kitchen.
MARWOOD: I'm not.
MONTY: Of course you are. Cooking's one of the natural
   instincts.
   He heads for him with the apron. MARWOOD *defends
   with his leg.*
MARWOOD: Listen Monty, this is all very kind of you, but

83

I really think I ought to get out there and get some work done on the car . . .

MONTY: Nonsense, you haven't time. We'll be having a late luncheon at three.

MARWOOD would say anything to avoid the apron. Says the first thing that comes into his head. It is said with great regret.

MARWOOD: 'Fraid we have to leave by three, Monty.

MONTY: Leave?

MARWOOD: Yes, didn't he tell you? We've gotta get back to sign on.

MONTY: Sign on? At a Labour Exchange?

But you're successful actors? They realise the blunder together.

MARWOOD: It's sort of fashionable, actually. All the actors do it. Even Redgrave.

MONTY: But surely you could forgo for just this one occasion? I've come a very long way to see you both.

MONTY's eyes bulge behind his glasses. MARWOOD *affects remorse.*

MARWOOD: Well, no. Can't really. I mean, I'd love to stay. But he's more adamant to get back than I am.

MONTY: Then we must choose our moment, and have a word with him. I'm sure together we could persuade him.

MARWOOD suddenly finds himself entering into some sort of pact.

Now slip this on.

MONTY has both the problem and MARWOOD in hand. The apron goes on. MARWOOD is tied up at the back and MONTY returns to his work.

Garlic, rosemary and salt. I can never touch meat until

it's cooked. As a youth I used to weep in butcher's
shops.

MARWOOD *transfers his meat to the table and
reluctantly begins a search for the condiments. Garlic
and salt come out. 'I can't find the rosemary.' Feigning
exasperation,* MONTY *launches beans at the sink and
approaches wiping his hands on the apron.* MARWOOD
attempts to get out of his way. Out of luck instead.
MONTY *circles him in his arms and forces him
backwards over the table. Their faces come to the
point where they normally kiss in films.*

MONTY: I'm sure we can find it together.

MARWOOD *continues to arc backwards as* MONTY
searches behind him.

MARWOOD: Perhaps it's in the other bag?

MONTY: Perhaps it is. Shall we look?

Before they do WITHNAIL *barges in. Dumps groceries
on the table.*

WITHNAIL: Oh – sorry. Sherry's in there.

*He gestures towards a carrier bag and continues into
the living room as though he'd disturbed the courting
couple.* MONTY *doesn't seem at all concerned. Breaks
away to deal with the sherry.* MARWOOD *follows*
WITHNAIL. *A fast and frenetic exchange of whispers.*

MARWOOD: What d'you mean 'sorry'? What's going on?
What's he doing here?

WITHNAIL *collapses into an armchair and begins
removing his bags.*

We can't stay. He won't leave me alone.

Further exchange is cut off by MONTY. *He lumbers in
with three glasses of differing style and an opened
bottle of Bristol Cream.*

MONTY: I'm afraid we must drink from these.

The glasses are handed out and MONTY *moves over them with sherry.*

I trust their shape will not offend your palate . . .

MONTY *slips the wink at* MARWOOD *and proposes an expansive toast.*

To a delightful weekend in the country.

The glasses go up. A clink. A drink. Everyone is happy but MARWOOD.

74. INT. JAG/MOUNTAINSIDE. TRACK. DAY.

Effortless sunlight. An amateur photographer's day.

MARWOOD *and* WITHNAIL *are in the process of salvaging the Jag.*

MARWOOD: You were the one who wanted to leave.

WITHNAIL: You were the one who wanted to stay.

MARWOOD: Well, we can't. You saw him. He practically kissed me.

WITHNAIL: All right, we'll get the lunch down and afterwards I'll have a word with him and we'll leave.

MONTY *appears from the house with a teasing remonstration.*

MONTY: You foolish boys. What on earth possessed you to bring a car up here?

He starts waving his arms about. Points to a parking spot.

Get it over there, and we'll travel in the Rolls.

75. EXT. COUNTRY ROAD. DAY.

With Charlie Kunz supplying the music the Roller winds down a hill. Boys in the back and Monty driving. A small country town appears in the distance.

MONTY (V.O.): I do think you could have shaved. What on earth will people think of me turning up with you two. You look like a pair of farm-hands.

76. EXT. MARKET SQUARE. PENRITH. DAY.
Surprise from the locals as everyone gets out. WITHNAIL *and* MARWOOD *with their dishevelled appearance.* MONTY *with his watch and waistcoat and radish in his lapel. Residents actually stop and stare.*

MONTY: This is most embarrassing. Let's get away from the car.
Beetling off he crosses the square with them following. MONTY *brakes and a wallet comes out. A pair of crisp blue notes are dispersed. He shoves a glance towards the Penrith Tea Rooms.*

MONTY: Buy the Wellingtons and I'm going to buy some razors and shaving soap, and I'll see you over there in half an hour.
And off he fucks. MARWOOD *examines the loot as* WITHNAIL *arrives.*

MARWOOD: Pair of blues. One each.
WITHNAIL *flexes his fiver and is infused with a sudden inspiration.*

WITHNAIL: I think a drink, don't you?
MARWOOD: What about the Wellingtons?
WITHNAIL: Bollocks to the Wellingtons.
They cross the cobbles, heading towards King Henry's public house.
We'll tell him they had a farmers' conference and had a run on them.

77. INT. KING HENRY'S PUB. SALOON BAR. DAY.
A dingy little establishment. WITHNAIL *sits alone at the bar in front of a pair of half-drunk pints. His eyes study a mirror reflecting* MARWOOD *making a telephone call half-way down a hallway. The receiver goes down and* MARWOOD *reappears looking despondent.*

MARWOOD: Hasn't heard a thing. Apparently they're still seeing people.

WITHNAIL: You don't wanna go to Manchester, anyway. Play a bloody soldier?

MARWOOD: Don't I? I damned well do. It's a damned good little theatre.

WITHNAIL: Not much of a part though, is it?

MARWOOD: Better than nothing.

WITHNAIL: They'd make you cut your hair off.

MARWOOD: So what. You'd lose a leg.

> WITHNAIL *finishes his pint. The* BARMAN *informs them* 'Time Gents.'

WITHNAIL: All right, we're gonna have to work quickly. A pair of quadruple whiskies, and another pair of pints please.

78. EXT. MARKET SQUARE. PENRITH. DAY.
Speed of consumption has affected speed of inebriation. WITHNAIL *shuffles up the pavement. A lack of Monty produces indignation.*

WITHNAIL: Where is he? I'm utterly arse-holed.

MARWOOD: We're early.

> *He nods towards the tea rooms on the other side of the square.*

We wanna get in there, don't we? Eat some cake. Soak up the booze.

79. INT. PENRITH TEA ROOMS. DAY.

A bell on a spring clatters above their heads. All eyes turn in their direction. Not an eyeball in here under seventy years old. Maybe five or six ladies eating dainty little cakes with dainty little forks. The place is dainty. Decorated like one of its iced and jujubed numbers in the window. An OLD WOMAN *in an apron approaches as* WITHNAIL *gestures towards a gingham-clothed table.*

WITHNAIL: All right here?

OLD WOMAN: What do you want?

WITHNAIL: Cake. All right here?

> *Clearly a pair of drunken dustmen. She shows considerable courage.*

OLD WOMAN: No. We're closing in a minute.

WITHNAIL: We're leaving in a minute.

> *They sit down and* WITHNAIL *studies the menu. An old man with a neck lagged in bandage like the top of a boiler glares at them.* WITHNAIL *ignores him and pokes a finger at the 'Afternoon Teas'.*

We'll have cake and tea.

> *The* BOILER *gets up, balancing on his walking stick.*

BOILER: Didn't you hear? She said she's closed.

> *Insubordination, and the* BOILER *approaches red of face.*

What do you want in here?

WITHNAIL: Cake. What's it to do with you?

BOILER: I happen to be the proprietor. Now would you leave?

WITHNAIL: Ah, I'm glad you're the proprietor. I was gonna have to have a word with you anyway. We're working on a film up here. Location see. We might wanna do a film in here.

BOILER: You're drunk.

MARWOOD: Just bring out the cakes.

WITHNAIL: Cakes and fine wines.

> *This is a desperate situation. But the* OLD WOMAN *has a solution.*

OLD WOMAN: If you don't leave, we'll call the police.

> *A threat that brings a flutter of agreement from the feathers in the hats and the pugs on leads faction.*

WITHNAIL: Balls. We want the finest wines available to humanity. And we want them *here*. And we want them *now*.

BOILER: Miss Blenehassitt. Telephone the police.

MARWOOD: All right, Miss Blenehassitt, I'm warning you. If you do, you're fired. We'll buy this place and fire you immediately. We're multi-millionaires . . .

> MARWOOD *and* WITHNAIL *rise to their feet and the* BOILER *steps back.*

WITHNAIL: Yes, we'll buy this place. And we'll get a fucking juke-box in here to liven all these stiffs up a bit.

BOILER: The police, Miss Blenehassitt.

> *She goes about it. Fumbles nervously with the phone. Bit of chat from the hats and pugs.* 'Vagabonds.' 'They won't like the police.'

Just say there are two drunks in the Penrith Tea Rooms and we want them removed.

MARWOOD: We're not drunks. We're multi-millionaires.

BOILER: Hurry up, Mabs. We'll keep them here till they arrive.

> *Seems like he's going to bolt the door. A whispered explanation.*

HAT AND PUG: He'll keep them talking.

WITHNAIL: He won't keep us anywhere. We'll buy this place and have it knocked down.

Just as Mabs says 'Police please' a limousine appears outside.

MARWOOD: Don't bother. Our car's arrived. We're going.

Eyes alternate between them and the car as they reach the door.

WITHNAIL: But we'll be back. We're coming back in here.

The BOILER *and the* OLD WOMAN *and the old* LADIES *with the feathers and dogs on leads watch in amazement as* WITHNAIL *and* MARWOOD *stagger out and slump in the back of an immaculate Rolls-Royce.*

80. INT. LIVING ROOM. COTTAGE. DAY.

The lamb is sizzling to perfection. WITHNAIL *draws air over his teeth. Closes the oven door.* MARWOOD *appears from the kitchen washed and shaved and drying his hair.*

MARWOOD: Where is he?

WITHNAIL: Sulking up the hill. He says he won't come in for lunch without an apology.

MARWOOD: Suits me. He can eat his fucking radish.

They sit in front of the fire. MARWOOD *cracks a bottle. He's filling the glasses when a voice hisses petulantly in his ear.*

MONTY (O.S.): It's all your fault.

MONTY straightens up with an expression of teasing indignation.

You lead him astray.

MARWOOD: I beg your pardon, Monty?

MONTY: Oh, don't tell me you're not aware of it. I know what you're up to, and so do you.

WITHNAIL *stands with the bottle. Fills a glass and proffers it.*

Sherry? Oh dear, no, no, no. I'd be sucked into his trap. One of us has got to stay on guard. He's so mauve. We don't know what he's planning.

MARWOOD's *expression makes it clear that if* WITHNAIL *participates in this particular tack he will be lunching alone.* WITHNAIL *doesn't participate. And* MARWOOD *escapes into the kitchen.*

81. INT. KITCHEN. COTTAGE. DAY.

Al Bowley scratching in the background. MARWOOD *is at the sink peeling potatoes.* MONTY *joins him at the draining board with his beans. Arse-holed on sherry and enjoying himself.*

MONTY: I'm preparing myself to forgive you . . .

And he closes on him with an intimate whisper.

I think you've been punished enough. (*Smiles*) I think we'd better release you from the *légumes*, and transfer your talents to the meat.

Clasping his hand MONTY *heads for the living room.* MARWOOD *manages to pull away and exchange it for another nervous smile.*

You shouldn't treat each other so badly. The boy's out here, frozen to the marrow, and you just sit in here drinking.

MONTY *manoeuvres* MARWOOD *to the fire and re-addresses* WITHNAIL.

Now come along. He's going to revitalise himself, and you're going to finish the vegetables.

WITHNAIL: I don't know how to do them.

MONTY: Of course you don't. You're incapable of indulging in anything but pleasure. Am I not right?

MONTY misinterprets MARWOOD's *smile as protection of* WITHNAIL.

You don't deserve such loyalty.

WITHNAIL *is prised to his feet and escorted into the kitchen.*

Come along. I'm going to teach you how to peel a potato.

MONTY rolls WITHNAIL's *sleeves up.* MARWOOD *staring after them. The geography of the room dislocates through a slow dissolve.*

82. INT. LIVING ROOM. COTTAGE. DAY.

WITHNAIL *has shaved and they are half-way through lunch.* MONTY *is going at it with a will. He empties a bottle of wine and dispatches* WITHNAIL *into the kitchen for a replacement. Despite a monstrous gobful of food, he manages a smile for* MARWOOD. *It's reciprocated. Not because he sees anything to smile at. But because embarrassment forces him to.* MONTY's *stares are hard enough to itch.* MARWOOD *looks relieved when* WITHNAIL *reappears with a bottle of wine.*

MONTY: Isn't it stimulating, getting back to a basic sort of life for a while?

WITHNAIL: Yes.

His fork plunges into a roast potato almost before he sits down.

MONTY: Surrounded by trees and nature, one feels a glorious stirring of the senses. A rejection of poisonous inhibition, and a fecund motion of the soul . . .

MARWOOD: Except of course the problems tend to take the edge off the pleasure. I mean, with no proper facilities.

MONTY: All the glorious trials of youth. When I was a lad I'd rocket off on my tandem with Wrigglesworth, and we'd just ride and ride. And at night, we'd find some barn, and fall asleep with the perfumes of nature sighing on our skin.

All this said staring at MARWOOD. *He responds with an awful begummed smile.* WITHNAIL *leans into* MONTY *with an air of delicacy.*

WITHNAIL: Would it be in bad form to plagiarise a toast?

MONTY: Depends entirely on the quality of the wine. In this instance, most certainly it would not.

WITHNAIL *tops up the glasses. They raise to the point of contact.*

WITHNAIL: In that case, to a delightful weekend in the country.

Both MONTY *and* MARWOOD *are decidedly surprised by the proposal.* MARWOOD *can't believe his ears and* MONTY *can't believe his luck. He draws* MARWOOD *into his pally conspiracy.*

MONTY: Splendid. We expected a volley of argument . . . concerning Mr Redgrave!

And here's one of them. MARWOOD's *voice is as brittle as glass.*

MARWOOD: You're forgetting Jake, aren't you?

MONTY: Not another word. Jake can wait too.

MARWOOD: Jake isn't a friend, Monty. I hoped to avoid telling you this, I didn't want to alarm you. But there's a psychotic on the prowl outside this house.

The news squashes appetite and pleasure. MONTY
turns to WITHNAIL.

Ask him whether I exaggerate. He's threatened us, and
he's dangerous.

MONTY: Is this true?

WITHNAIL *lowers his fork. Throws away a light smile.
Dilutes it.*

WITHNAIL: Well, there's this local type hanging about. A
poacher. Got into a tiff with him, and he threatened
me with a dead fish.

*His tone proves there are different ways of telling the
truth.*

Yes, it was rather amusing actually. When you came
in, we thought it was him. And we thought you
scraping your boots was him sharpening his knife.

MONTY: Oh, how delicious . . .

Absolutely fucking hilarious. MARWOOD *can't take
any more of this. Fun reverts to feeding.* MONTY
*beams across with his utensils poised over the lamb as
though about to play a tune on it.*

More meat?

MARWOOD: No thanks. I'm going for some air.

83. EXT. GARDENS. COTTAGE. DAY.

MARWOOD *sits next to the little stream. The sun is setting.
The kind of visuals that get into adverts.* WITHNAIL
approaches from the cottage smoking a Turkish cigarette.

WITHNAIL: I know what you're thinking, but I had no
alternative. Old bugger's come a long way, and I
didn't wanna put the wind up him.

MARWOOD: Your sensitivity overwhelms me. And if you
think you're gonna get a weekend's indulgence up here

at his expense, which'll mean him having a weekend's
indulgence up here at my expense, you've got another
think coming.

WITHNAIL: I give you my word, we'll leave first thing
tomorrow morning.

MARWOOD: Tomorrow? Tomorrow? What about
tonight?

WITHNAIL: He's not gonna try anything . . .

MARWOOD: Of course he is. Why d'you think he's up
here? He means business.

WITHNAIL *attempts to lighten the situation.*
Prevaricating. And concealing it.

WITHNAIL: Anyway, he sent me out to tell you the coffee's
ready.

MARWOOD: I couldn't drink it. I've got cramp in the
mouth from grinning.

WITHNAIL: Well stop smiling at him.

MARWOOD: I can't help it. I'm so uptight with him, I
can't stop myself.

84. INT. LIVING ROOM. COTTAGE. EVENING.

WITHNAIL *is drinking coffee.* MARWOOD *is staring into his*
cup. MONTY *is arse-holed and on his feet and emoting at*
the ceiling.

MONTY: *Laisse-moi respirer, longtemps longtemps l'odeur*
de tes cheveux. Ah, Baudelaire. Brings back such
memories of Oxford. Oh, Oxford.
The orbs refocus. He heads for the tub with the
walking sticks.
Halcyon days. The gentle ego making art. The brutes'
selfishness.

85. EXT. MOUNTAINSIDE. OVER LAKE. EVENING.
A massive panorama with three tiny figures in the far distance.

MARWOOD (V.O.): Followed by yet another anecdote about his sensitive crimes in a punt with a chap called Norman who had red hair and a book of poetry stained with butter drips from crumpets.

86. EXT. TRACT. MOUNTAINSIDE. EVENING.
A pair of field glasses slung round his neck. A walking stick in his fist. Intoxicated with alcohol. Or the gloaming. Or both. MONTY *leads down the track with* WITHNAIL *and* MARWOOD *following.*

MONTY: I often wonder where Norman is now. Probably wintering with his mother in Guildford. A cat and rain. Vim under the sink. And both bars on.
He turns towards the lake. Hits a sheep with some Latin.

MONTY (*in Latin*): . . . but *old* now . . . old . . . There can be no true beauty without decay.

WITHNAIL (*in Latin*): A requiem for England.
MARWOOD *doesn't understand this. Doesn't like the sound of it.*

MONTY: How right you are. How right you are. We live in a kingdom of rains where royalty comes in gangs. Come on lads, let's get home. The sky's beginning to bruise, night will fall, and we'll be forced to camp.
He takes off down the track. MARWOOD *forcefully detains* WITHNAIL.

MARWOOD: He's having your bed, all right? That's the condition, all right?

WITHNAIL: All right.

MARWOOD: I want the room with the lock. Agree to that, or I'm off.

WITHNAIL: All right. All right.

The cottage emerges from behind a knoll of rock. About sixty yards away. A suspicious figure is moving in the gloom of the gardens. The view stops WITHNAIL *in his tracks.* JAKE *is back. The news is instantly communicated to* MONTY. *Also stops in his tracks. Everyone is concerned. Except* MARWOOD *who's delighted.*

MARWOOD: Good old Jake, eh? I told you, he's back. And that's precisely the reason I'm off to London.

No Old Vic when we feel like it now. WITHNAIL *has the wind up. He stares at* MONTY *who squints through binoculars towards the house.*

Let's all have a good laugh, eh, Withnail? Old Jake's back, eh?

MONTY: He's on his way. He's leaving.

MARWOOD takes command. WITHNAIL *and* MONTY *follow him.*

MARWOOD: Come on, let's pack up. We'll get out of here before it gets dark.

87. EXT. COURTYARD. COTTAGE. EVENING.

The gloom thickens. Mostly in MONTY. *They creep the yard and discover a hare hanging on the back door accompanied by a note. 'Here. Hare. Here. Jake.' Suddenly everyone is back on holiday. Except* MARWOOD. *They vanish inside.*

88. INT. BOUDOIR. COTTAGE. NIGHT.

Candlelight and a blazing fire. A good Bordeaux and celery and Stilton. Ivor Novello singing 'We'll Gather Lilacs' on the gramophone. This could be 1932.

MARWOOD *looks worried.* WITHNAIL *looks drunk.* MONTY *looks artful. They are playing seven-card-draw poker. Half-crowns and bottle tops.* MONTY *bets from his stack.* MONTY *is encouraging* WITHNAIL *to drink while* MARWOOD's *glass is filled under protest. The only thing he gets from* MONTY *is smiles. Uptight. No smiles back. There's something going on here. And* MARWOOD *doesn't like the cut of it. Maybe it's imagination but* WITHNAIL *and* MONTY *seem prepared to giggle for the most trivial of reasons.* MONTY *deals the cards with a quip for* MARWOOD's *patently bad hand.*

MONTY (*in Latin*): Looking a bit lonely, isn't he?
WITHNAIL (*in Latin*): He needs a queen to come to the
    rescue.

> MONTY's *mouth puckers with mirth. A queen for* MARWOOD! *It hits like a punch line. Creases* MONTY *and he and* WITHNAIL *simmer in amusement.* MARWOOD *isn't amused. Face like a rock. Bets are placed. The room loses focus via a dissolve.*

89. INT. BOUDOIR. COTTAGE. NIGHT.
MONTY *is cranking at the gramophone. Both the Pernod and candles have gone down several inches. A huge stack of beer-bottle tops and half-crowns in front of* WITHNAIL.

> *He is ferociously drunk.* MONTY *returns to the table.* WITHNAIL's *deal. He can't make it.*

> MARWOOD *immediately gets up. Manoeuvres* WITHNAIL *to the couch. But the bastard's reneged. Offers resistance. Wants to go upstairs.*

MONTY: I think we'd better get him to bed.

MARWOOD: No, no. He's down here. You're in my room. I'm in his room. And he's down here.

MONTY: I wouldn't dream of depriving the poor fellow of his bed. And especially in that condition.

MARWOOD: It's agreed. It's what he wants.

WITHNAIL: No I don't. I wanna get to bed.

And that's precisely where he's heading. Despite MARWOOD's *efforts, he barges for the stairs.* MARWOOD *adopts a sort of instant homosexuality. Dripping wrists and a pink voice.*

MARWOOD: All right then, lovey. Come on. Let's get you to bed. Early night'll do us good. Night, night, then Monty.

A convoy heads up the stairs. WITHNAIL *gurgles as they climb.*

WITHNAIL: I wanna be alone. I wanna be alone.

90. INT. TOP OF STAIRS. COTTAGE. NIGHT.

His chances are slim. MARWOOD *has turned into some kind of nancy boy. The theory is sleep with* WITHNAIL *equals safety. The landing creaks under* MONTY's *feet.* MARWOOD *has become quite lovey dovey.*

MARWOOD: Thank you Monty. We're all right now. I've got a candle in here.

Cradling WITHNAIL *he leads him into the bedroom. Dumps the vile corpse on his bed.* MONTY's *still at the door as* MARWOOD *flits out.*

I'll say good night now, Monty.

He wafts past into his bedroom. Makes the bed in under four seconds. Grabs item of underwear. Heads back for WITHNAIL's *room.*

Huge shadows in the lamplight. MONTY *has just locked*

WITHNAIL's *door. Key into the pocket. Mr Badger and Mr Mole.* MARWOOD *is horrified. Instantly an ex-homosexual.* MONTY *doesn't seem to notice.*

MONTY: I think he'd better sleep alone tonight.

MARWOOD's *mind races. But his feet won't move. He stutters back.*

He doesn't want to sleep with you.

MARWOOD: All right then. You're in there. I'll get a blanket. I'll have the couch.

His disappearance into the bedroom is so brief it isn't worth mentioning. He re-appears. Passes MONTY. *Descends the stairs.*

I'll say good night, then.

MONTY: You've already said it. Twice.

He doesn't say it again. Hot foots it through the stairwell door.

91. INT. BOUDOIR. COTTAGE. NIGHT.

MARWOOD *closes the door behind him. It opens again almost instantly.* MONTY *expands into the room. Deals gently with the latch.*

MARWOOD: What is it, Monty? I'm very tired. I need to go to sleep.

MONTY's *fluids are on the move. He glides gently round the room.*

MONTY: But not that tired, eh?

Apparently he is. Starts making his bed up. MONTY *closes on him.*

MONTY: Are you a sponge or a stone?

MARWOOD: What d'you mean?

MONTY: D'you like to experience all facets of life, or do you shut yourself off from new experience?

MARWOOD: I voted Conservative.

MONTY: Are you faithful?

MARWOOD: To whom?

MONTY: Faithfulness isn't selective.

MARWOOD: No, I quite agree. It's more a question of selecting to whom one will be faithful.

MONTY: Have you selected?

MARWOOD: I'm terribly tired.

MONTY: I've been watching you all evening. You've been avoiding my eyes, haven't you?

As off-handedly as possible in reference to these bulbous spheres.

MARWOOD: Your eyes?

MARWOOD's *legs quiver like a gnat's legs in death throes. Tries to articulate but can't.*

MONTY: At luncheon you could hardly take your gaze from mine. This evening you've hardly looked at me.

He's looking at him now. In alarm.

What did he say to you?

MARWOOD: Nothing.

MONTY: You can tell me, you know.

MARWOOD: I assure you, nothing. Look here, Monty, I really must go to bed.

MONTY *constructs a smile. And then separates it with his tongue.*

MONTY: Yes. You must. Mustn't you.

Suddenly his waistcoat is off. Also bow tie.

Off you go then. I shall sleep here. Won't be the first time I've been left with the couch.

MARWOOD *wears diving boots to the door. A second later he's gone.*

102

92. INT. BEDROOM. COTTAGE. NIGHT.

All the usual noises of the night. A door banging in the wind. An owl hooting five miles away. A footstep on the bottom stair.

The room is pitch black. Just a hint of light through the window. The footsteps continue to mount. Slow heavy treads. If MARWOOD *is asleep when they begin he's awake by the time they reach his door.*

The door knob turns. A chair holds it for a while. Then fractures slowly under the determination of the intruder. Panic in the dark. He is in. MARWOOD *has no defence other than to pretend to be asleep.*

MONTY: Boy. Boy. I know you're not asleep. Boy.

MONTY *moves to the bed. Sits at the end. His voice is quivering.*

But he is. I've been into his room. He won't hear a thing.

A key descends on the bedside table. Owls hooting and snoring.

I know you're not asleep, boy.

MARWOOD: No, I'm not, Monty. What do you want?

He snaps up. A match strikes. A candle lights. Horror. 'Good God in heaven.' A huge woman is sitting at the end of the bed.

MONTY: I had to come. I tried not to. Oh, how I tried not to.

MONTY *isn't actually in drag. First glance and the outfit looks like drag. Long paisley silk dressing gown and velvet slippers. Little bit of make up. Nothing ostentatious. A smudge of rouge.*

MARWOOD: Look here, Monty. There's something I have to explain to you.

MONTY: You needn't explain. He's told me everything. He told me that first day you came to Chelsea.

MARWOOD: What? What did he tell you?

MONTY: He told me about your arrest in the Tottenham Court Road. He told me about your problems. How you feel. Your desires.

MARWOOD: What problems?

MONTY: You are a toilet trader.

MARWOOD: He told you that?

MONTY somehow manages to motor quickly up the bed on his arse.

MONTY: You mustn't blame him, and you mustn't blame yourself. I know how you feel, and how difficult it is. And that's why you mustn't hold back, ruin your youth as I nearly did over Eric. It's like a tide. Give in to it boy. Go with it. Its society's crime. Not ours.

MARWOOD: I'm not homosexual, Monty.

MONTY: Yes you are. Of course you are. You're simply blackmailing your emotions to avoid the realities of your relationship with him.

MARWOOD: What are you talking about?

MONTY: You love him. And it isn't his fault he cannot love you, any more than it is my fault that I adore you.

That'll do for MARWOOD. He leaps from the bed. Cloaks himself in a blanket and bolts for the door. MONTY is as fast as he is.

Couldn't we allow ourselves just this one moment of indiscretion?

MARWOOD: No.

MONTY: He would never know.

MARWOOD: I don't care what he knows. You've gotta go, Monty. You gotta get out.

He tries to open the door to get out himself.

MONTY isn't having it. MARWOOD *is inhibited with fear of dropping the blanket. Bit of a scuffle. He rushes across the room with* MONTY *in pursuit. His impassioned voice rises with an overload of emotion.*

MONTY: If you want to humiliate me, humiliate me. I adore you.

MARWOOD backs off. MONTY *nails him into a corner. An owl hoots.*

Tell him if you must. I no longer care. I mean to have you . . . even if it must be burglary.

A rapid and almost indecipherable series of protests from MARWOOD. *All to no effect. Not much light to see what's happening. But lips seek lips. A sheer expanse of bosom makes resistance impossible.* MARWOOD *takes what he can. Grabs* MONTY's *ear and screams at him.*

MARWOOD: It's not me. It's him. He lied to you. We're an affair. Have been for years. But he doesn't want you to know. Doesn't want anyone to know.

MONTY seems to deflate a little. MARWOOD *still clings to an ear.*

We're both in it. We're obsessed with each other. But he's ashamed. *Ashamed.* He refuses to come out and accept what he is. That's why he's rejecting me while you're here.

The owls hooting. Two naked men in a corner. The bubble bursts.

On my life, Monty. This is the first night we haven't

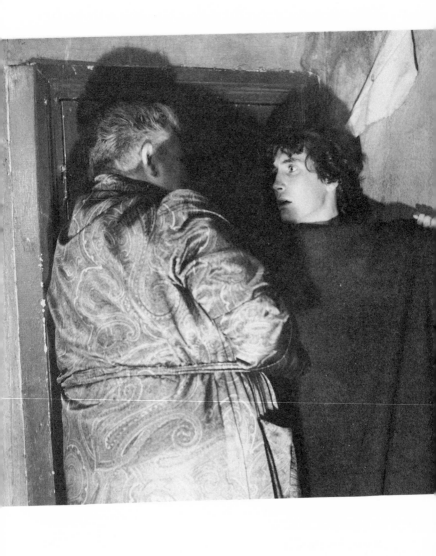

slept together in six years. I can't cheat on him. It
would kill him.

MONTY: He told me you were in purgatory because he
couldn't love you.

MARWOOD: He's lying. Lying.

*A moment later they are retogged in their respective
garments.*

MONTY: Oh, my boy. Had I known I'd never have
attempted to come between you.

MARWOOD: I know that, Monty. I respect you for your
sensitivity.

A period of sterile atmospherics. MARWOOD *hastens
to the door.*

I thank you for it. But you must leave.

MONTY: Yes. Yes. You'd better go to him.

MARWOOD: I intend to. This instant.

93. INT. BEDROOM. COTTAGE. NIGHT.

The door flies open. MARWOOD *barges in. Y-fronts and an
oil lamp.*

MARWOOD: Withnail. You bastard. Wake up.

WITHNAIL'S *forty-a-day tongue hangs from his mouth.
Jewelled with a morbid sequin of spittle. His snoring
enrages the man in pants.*

Wake up. You bastard. Or I'll burn the fucking bed
down.

*He moves in with his lamp. A voice muffled with sleep
and blankets.*

WITHNAIL: I deny all accusations. What do you want?

MARWOOD *grabs his shroud of overcoat and blankets.
Wrenches them to the floor.* WITHNAIL *stirs. A waxy
body and shotgun revealed.*

MARWOOD: I've just narrowly avoided having a buggering. I've come in here with the express intention of wishing one on you. Having said that, I'm now going to leave for London.

WITHNAIL *regards this threat with enough seriousness to sit up.*

WITHNAIL: Hold on. Don't wanna let your imagination run away with you.

MARWOOD: *Imagination.* I've just finished fighting a naked man. How dare you tell him I'm a toilet trader.

WITHNAIL: It was a tactical necessity.

WITHNAIL *scratches his head into focus. Makes an inspection of the candle saucer. Finds a dog end. Lights it. A deep inhalation.*

If I hadn't told him you were active, we'd never have got the cottage.

MARWOOD: I'd never have wanted it. Not with him in it.

A whine of rattling mucus. An evil cough. WITHNAIL *stubs the dog.*

WITHNAIL: God. That hurt. I never thought he'd come all this way.

MARWOOD: *Monty?* He'd go to *New York.*

WITHNAIL: A calculated risk.

MARWOOD: What is all this tactical necessity and calculated risk? This is me naked in a corner. And how *dare* you tell him I love you? And how *dare you* tell him you rejected me?

An almost imperceptible smile stagnates on WITHNAIL's *mouth.*

How *dare you* tell him that?

WITHNAIL: Sorry about that. I got a bit carried away, sort of said it without thinking.

107

MARWOOD: Well let me tell you something, Withnail. If he comes into my room again, it's murder.
He grabs the shotgun. Heads for the door. Speaks before the slam.
MARWOOD: And you'll be held responsible in law.

94. EXT. VALLEY. OVER LAKE. DAY.
A big view. Sunlight through thunder clouds. Black edged with gold. Lightning on the horizon. A rumble of thunder. Both it and Crow Crag are several miles away. MARWOOD's *voice seeps in over the cottage.*
MARWOOD (V.O.): . . . and I could not help but hear your unfortunate exchange which I believe was ostensibly caused by me. I do assure you it was not my intention. Nor, may I add, did I expect to bid so empty a valediction as that which circumstances necessitate.

95. INT. LIVING ROOM. COTTAGE. DAY.
WITHNAIL *is up to his elbows in lunch. Cold lamb. Hot potatoes. Plenty of enthusiasm and wine. All in all things have turned out rather well.* MARWOOD *sits opposite reading from Monty's note.*
MARWOOD: Perhaps it is appropriate justice for the eavesdropper that he should leave as his trade determines, in secrecy and in the dead of night. I am, yours ever faithfully. Montague H. Withnail.
An instant of lightning. MARWOOD *crumples the note for the fire.*
Poor old bastard.
WITHNAIL *charges his maw with lamb. Talks through a mouthful.*

108

WITHNAIL: I would say that represents a degree of hypocrisy I have hitherto suspected in you but not noticed due to highly evasive skills.

A grand slam of thunder. A moment later it's pissing a monsoon.

MARWOOD: By Christ, Withnail. You'll suffer for this. What you've done will have to be paid for.

WITHNAIL goes about his grub with a grin. Examines the wine label.

WITHNAIL: I'll say one thing for Monty. He keeps a sensational cellar.

A toast to Monty is offered. Interrupted by a knock on the door. Infinite possibilities. Has Monty come back? MARWOOD walks into the kitchen. WITHNAIL staring after him. Opens the back door. A dishevelled POSTMAN outside. A telegram handed across. MARWOOD closes the door. Opens the envelope. Returns to the living room. WITHNAIL's turn to read the telegram. A smile. Without charity.

WITHNAIL: Well done.

MARWOOD: Doesn't mean to say I've got it – probably just wanna see me again.

High-voltage lightning.

Well, that settles it then.

WITHNAIL's mouth takes a stuffing. MARWOOD fights back yawns.

We're gonna have to leave immediately.

WITHNAIL: What?

MARWOOD: Get your kit together, I'm leaving in half an hour.

And he heads for the stairs, with WITHNAIL mouthing after him.

WITHNAIL: Half an hour? Don't be ridiculous. I need at least an hour for lunch.

96. EXT. MOTORWAY. NIGHT.
Not much traffic about. Thick rain keeps the Jag around seventy.

WITHNAIL (V.O.): You got a truck coming up. 'Bout two hundred yards, followed by a slow right hander.

MARWOOD (V.O.): I can't keep this up. This is insanity.

97. INT. JAGUAR SEDAN/MOTORWAY. NIGHT.
WITHNAIL *has virtually transferred the dining table to his lap. Here is the leg of lamb. Potatoes. Knife and fork. Bordeaux. And a bottle of gin.* MARWOOD's *vision is almost entirely obscured. He has to depend on* WITHNAIL *who navigates between mouthfuls.*

WITHNAIL: Stay in this lane. Bear right.

MARWOOD: What lane? I can't see the fucking lane.

WITHNAIL: Bear right. Bear right.

Tail lights of the truck. A near miss. That dreadful sound of a hooter being absorbed by speed. MARWOOD *takes an unnerving.*

MARWOOD: Right. That's it. Next garage I gotta find a windscreen wiper. Plus I gotta get some sleep.
WITHNAIL *doesn't seem concerned. Cackles through a hit of gin.*

98. EXT. MOTORWAY SERVICE AREA. NIGHT.
This is a tourist frightener. A giant boiled egg announces the name of the dump. Not much action. The Jag cruises in looking for the garage section. There isn't one. MARWOOD *pulls over.*

99. INT. JAGUAR/CAR PARK. SERVICE AREA. NIGHT.
MARWOOD *kills the engine. Yawns. Exhausted. Runs hands through his hair.* WITHNAIL *continues his dinner. Rain batters the roof.*
MARWOOD: Wake me when it stops.
> *He finds pills in the glove compartment. Starts climbing his seat.*
WITHNAIL: What am I supposed to do?
> MARWOOD *gets in the back of the car. Stretches along the seat.*
MARWOOD: Finish your dinner and drop a Surmontil.
> MARWOOD *grabs the gin bottle. Sinks a mouthful to take his pill.*

100. INT. JAGUAR SEDAN/STREETS. WEST LONDON. DAWN.
Mr Hendrix is once again responsible for this music. It cuts to the sequence so brilliantly it is pointless to attempt a description – although one word might help – anarchy.

MARWOOD *is stretched on the back seat. Intermittent patches of orange light wash his face. He wakes slowly. Looks up at the street lights whizzing by. A moment to work it out? Still in the back seat? The car's going like the clappers? But he isn't driving it! Fighting a pill-over he sits and looks over the seat.* WITHNAIL *is at the wheel trying to ram a cripple car!*

But it isn't a cripple car. It's one of those three-wheeled bubble things with a name like a plateful of spaghetti (Isoterra?). There's a lot coming into focus at once. (1) WITHNAIL *is drunk. (2) He hasn't got a licence. (3) There's a terrified middle-aged woman in this glass bubble*

111

trying to escape. (4) The Jaguar sounds fucked. (5) They're
roaring down a slope under the Chiswick flyover.

MARWOOD: What's going on?

WITHNAIL: I'm trying to ram this bastard.

> MARWOOD *directs eyes at the quarry. She's revving to*
> *get away.*

Watch her. Watch her.

MARWOOD: Are you out of your mind? Pull over. You
haven't got a licence.

WITHNAIL: No.

> *Huge close up of the chrome Jaguar. Now it's roaring*
> *up a slope and on to the M4. Despite* WITHNAIL's
> *effort the three-wheeler has superior acceleration and*
> *pulls away.*

See. We're being overtaken by everything on four
wheels. This bastard's aged ten thousand miles in four
hundred.

MARWOOD: Where are we?

WITHNAIL: London.

> *The engine beats like a flabby drum. Firing on only*
> *three cylinders.* WITHNAIL *floors the accelerator. Forty*
> *is about maximum. He hasn't got the mirror together.*
> *Turns back over his shoulder.*

Here comes another fucker.

> *The other fucker pulls alongside. Two faces stare into*
> *the Jag. They are both wearing identical hats. They*
> *are both* POLICEMEN.

MARWOOD: Oh no.

WITHNAIL: It's perfectly all right. Leave them to me.

MARWOOD: You're full of gin you silly tool.

> *Instructions to pull over are issued. The cops park*
> *their van in front of them and get out. As they walk*

towards the Jag WITHNAIL *hides bottles. A fat face appears at the window.*

WITHNAIL *doesn't open it. A black-leather-clad knuckle taps.* MARWOOD *issues another* 'Oh no.' *And* WITHNAIL *winds the window down. Nothing is said for a moment. Government eyes scan the bottles. From anyone's point of view this doesn't look good. From a policeman's point of view it looks fucking wonderful. One in the front. Bearded. Clearly drunk. One in the back. Bearded. Clearly drugged.*

POLICEMAN: Bit early in the morning for festivities, isn't it?

WITHNAIL: These aren't mine. They belong to him.

POLICEMAN: You're drunk.

WITHNAIL: I assure you I'm not, Officer. Honestly. I've only had a few ales.

POLICEMAN TWO *examines a front tyre. Sees his reflection in it.*

POLICEMAN: Out of the car. Please. Sir.

101. EXT. CARRIAGEWAY/JAGUAR. SUBURBS. DAWN.

WITHNAIL *and* MARWOOD *get out. All the usual terror. Radios going. Lights flashing. Job satisfaction. Here comes a breath kit.*

POLICEMAN: I want you to take one deep breath and fill this bag.

WITHNAIL *looks at the bag. Looks at the copper. Shakes his head.*

POLICEMAN: Are you refusing to fill this bag?

WITHNAIL: I most certainly am.

POLICEMAN: I'm placing you under arrest.

WITHNAIL: Don't be ridiculous. I haven't done anything.

The back of the van is opened. WITHNAIL *is hustled towards it.*

Look here. My cousin's a QC.

POLICEMAN TWO *turns into a Nazi. Extraordinarily high-pitched.*

POLICEMAN: Get in the back of the van.

WITHNAIL *gets in the back of the van. Promptly.* MARWOOD *joins him.*

102. INT. POLICE STATION. DAY.

A green wall with a cream stripe around it. The room is full of uniforms. WITHNAIL *is handed a sort of bottle and instructed to piss in it. The* ARRESTING OFFICER *escorts him to a corner where he is surrounded with curtains. The sorts of thing that go round hospital beds. Forms are getting filled in at a desk.* MARWOOD *looks at his watch. The constabulary receives tea in mugs.*

These boys are paid to be suspicious. And they are. POLICEMAN TWO *approaches the curtains. He wants to know if* WITHNAIL *has 'done'. Evidently he hasn't. The curtains are pulled aside and* MARWOOD *gets a view.* WITHNAIL *stares back. Suspicion increases as he turns away. Left arm pumping like a chicken's wing.* MARWOOD *suddenly realises what's happening. The device! The* POLICEMAN *doesn't know what's happening. But knows something is afoot. Pulls his prisoner round. Here's something for the* Police Gazette! *Six inches of transparent plastic tube hang from* WITHNAIL's *zip. A valve on the end of it like a tiny tap. As the cop comprehends what he's staring at this valve delivers. Now* WITHNAIL's *trying to turn it off. Danny should stick to dolls.*

103. EXT. STREET. LONDON. DAY.
A bright sunny day. Cotton wool clouds. Trees in leaf.
Flowers. A luxury new development of apartments.
Penthouses at the top. But all this is to come. Right now
the street is dirty and dingy and in the middle of winter.
The Jaguar turns in. Parks opposite the huge architects'
billboard. The only sunny day around here.

The warehouse has been demolished. They hardly seem
to notice. Flashing lights all over the pavement. The first
wave of wankers arriving at site. They get out and vanish
into their house.

104. INT. HALLWAY/STAIRWAY. APARTMENT. DAY.
Stagger into the hallway. Utterly wasted. WITHNAIL *makes*
an inspection of the mail. A considerable amount of crap.
But no National Assistance payments. This is serious. He
looks at MARWOOD.
WITHNAIL: Where's our cheques?
MARWOOD: We didn't sign on.
   The house is divided into two apartments. Theirs is on
   the upper level. MARWOOD *unlocks the front door.*
   WITHNAIL *follows upstairs.*
WITHNAIL: That wouldn't make any difference to last
   week's payment.
   They've reached the bathroom door. Definitely someone
   in there! Half alarmed and half coming-on-brave
   MARWOOD *barges in. A vast* BLACK MAN *occupies the*
   bath. About three hundred pounds and as black as your
   hat. MARWOOD *looks at him and he looks back.*
   Nothing said and MARWOOD *quits the bathroom and*
   looks at WITHNAIL. *Still nothing said and* MARWOOD *is*
   now clattering upstairs. Pushes into a room at the top.

115

105. INT. BEDROOM. APARTMENT. DAY.

Pitch black. MARWOOD *gropes round the bed to get to the window. He tears the curtain apart. An animal on the bed. He jumps back. It's some sort of fox. A moment later a tranquillised man sits up.*

MARWOOD: What are you doing in my bed?

DANNY *scratches. Mutters something about sleep.*

MARWOOD *is angry.*

MARWOOD: Who's that huge spade in the bath?

DANNY: Presuming Ed.

MARWOOD: All right, you got ten minutes and I want you out . . . 'cause I wanna get in . . . ten minutes, and you better be on your feet.

106. INT. LIVING ROOM. APARTMENT. DAY.

WITHNAIL *is down on the couch with a bottle going.* MARWOOD *has a glass* WITHNAIL *attempts to refill. He refuses it and seems distinctly anxious. Stands and opens the curtains. A stretch in the country and this place is a shock. Smells like a tube station. Air cooked with ashtrays. Just like they left it. The door opens and* DANNY *comes in. Wears his pelt and a school satchel.*

WITHNAIL: How did you get in?

DANNY: Ingenuity, man. Come up the drainpipe.

DANNY *slings his pelt on the floor. It's a mangy brown fox with glass eyes. A grandmother's garment.*

Would you like a smoke?

WITHNAIL: Yes.

MARWOOD: No thanks. I gotta make a call.

He walks to the window, looking at his watch. Evidently still too early. DANNY *unloads his rolling*

116

*equipment. A bag of grass and Rizla papers. He begins
tearing out a stream of the latter.*

WITHNAIL: What are you gonna do with those?

DANNY: The joint I'm about to roll requires a craftsman.
It can utilise up to twelve skins. It is called a
Camberwell carrot.

MARWOOD *turns away from the window.* DANNY *is
applying the spittle.*

MARWOOD: It is impossible to use twelve papers on one
joint.

DANNY: It's impossible to make a Camberwell carrot with
anything less.

WITHNAIL: Who says it's a Camberwell carrot?

DANNY: I do. I invented it in Camberwell and it looks like
a carrot.

DANNY *introduces* WITHNAIL*'s nostrils to the grass.*
'A good bouquet.' *The answer is yes. But* WITHNAIL*'s
attention is with* MARWOOD. *He's nervous about his
call. And his nerves are making* WITHNAIL *nervous.*

DANNY: D'you realise this gaff's overrun with rodents?

A vibration from outside. MARWOOD *gets to his feet
again. He looks across the street. A hydraulic hammer
is in action on the building site opposite. More
wankers are arriving. And* DANNY *begins to roll.*
When I come in I seen one the siza fuckin' dog.

MARWOOD: No, that is a dog. It belongs to the fellow
downstairs.

DANNY: Does his dog get in the oven?

MARWOOD: No. His dog doesn't come up here.

DANNY: Then it was a rodent. Opened the oven door, and
it was in there lookin' at me. Quite freaked me at the
time. I was gonna cook onions.

117

MARWOOD's *watch is getting more attention. Figures it's late enough to make his move. Coat on and he heads for the door.*

Are you goin' to bed now?

MARWOOD: No. Phone.

He leaves with WITHNAIL's *eyes following. His thoughts are almost visible. A good chance* MARWOOD's *scored work. What happens then? Doesn't bear thinking about. But he's thinking about it.*

DANNY: Who's he gone to telephone?

WITHNAIL: Squat Betty.

He stands and walks to the window. Stares across the street. A phone booth opposite. WITHNAIL's *P.O.V.* MARWOOD *walks inside.* WITHNAIL *returns to the couch. Swallows wine and clarifies himself.*

WITHNAIL: His agent. But he's wasting his time 'cause he won't be in.

107. INT. (ANOTHER ANGLE). LIVING ROOM. APARTMENT. DAY.

PRESUMING ED *sits on the sofa. Seeing as he's not saying much I'm not saying much about him except he's really absolutely huge. Got a pair of vast 'Loons' on the size of tents. Got a tiny red-leather beatle cap on top of his big head like a pimple.*

Music – maybe? The Camberwell carrot is completed. DANNY *lights it and fills lungs. A drag or two later it's handed to* WITHNAIL.

DANNY: This'll tend to make you very high.

This Camberwell carrot represents perfection of the joint roller's art. An amalgamation of a toilet-roll tube and an ice-cream cone stuffed with dope. WITHNAIL

118

inhales with respect. Slaps a hand over his mouth to prevent his lungs rejecting the exhaust.

This grass is the most powerful in the western hemisphere. I have it specially flown in from my man in Mexico. He's an expert. His name's Juan. This grass grows at exactly two thousand feet above sea level.

MARWOOD *walks in in the middle of this crap. The carrot is back on its way to* DANNY. *Both look up.* WITHNAIL's *eyes interrogate. But* DANNY *asks the question.*

Did you get the part, man?

MARWOOD: No.

WITHNAIL's *spirits instantly rise.* DANNY *hands* MARWOOD *the joint.*

MARWOOD: I got a different one.

MARWOOD *seems in a state of virtual shock. Takes a deep hit on the joint without much realisation of it. Speaks via a lungful.*

MARWOOD: They want me to play the lead.

A moment of eye contact with WITHNAIL. *Aware of the potential hurt. But* WITHNAIL *smiles* 'Congratulations' *and reaches for the joint.*

DANNY: Where exactly have you two been?

MARWOOD: Holiday in the countryside.

DANNY: That's a very good idea. London is a country comin' down from its trip. We are sixty days from the enda this decade, and there's gonna be a lota refugees. We're about to witness the world's biggest hangover, and there's fuck all Harold Wilson can do about it.

The carrot glows in WITHNAIL's *mouth as he inhales.*

They'll be goin' round this town shoutin' 'Bring out your dead.'

The joint is handed back to its creator. DANNY *addresses* MARWOOD.

There was a geezer round here the other day looking for you.

MARWOOD: What geezer?

DANNY: Some bald geezer. Reckons you own him two hundred and sixty six quid back rent. I told him, there's no questiona payin' rent for a property cut with rodents.

PRESUMING ED *passes the joint to* MARWOOD *who sucks it cautiously.*

He takes exception to this, and comes on really bald with me.

WITHNAIL: What d'you mean, 'ratty'?

WITHNAIL *has amused himself. Starts to chuckle.*

DANNY *is serious.*

DANNY: I told him to piss off.

A hydraulic hammer starts barking with rabies on the building site.

MARWOOD: You bloody fool. He'll have us in court again.

DANNY: No he won't. It ain't legal.

WITHNAIL: I assume we can quote you, can we?

WITHNAIL *is still amused.* DANNY *replies with deadly sincerity.*

DANNY: Law rather appeals to me actually.

WITHNAIL *stares at him. He looks like a stoned sheep. The valve of credibility blows in* WITHNAIL's *brain. Laughter' and smoke explode from his face.* DANNY *looks at him. Their eyes meet.* WITHNAIL *falls off the sofa. Rolls hysterically with harsh giggles.*

DANNY *raises a foot to allow him to pass. Retrieves the carrot. Looks towards the raving hysteric at his feet without expression.*

DANNY: Just high.

And so is MARWOOD. *Though he disguises it he isn't enjoying it.*

MARWOOD: Stop laughing. This is serious.

DANNY: No it ain't. I looked into it.

DANNY takes a hit. Offers it to MARWOOD. *This time it's refused.*

I studied the papers.

MARWOOD: What papers?

DANNY: Legal papers.

WITHNAIL is crying with laughter. Manages enough air to speak.

WITHNAIL: He can appear for me. And I've got another case pending. He can fight both for me.

Another rictus of laughter. WITHNAIL *tries to crawl away from the table. Fails and falls on his gut.*

MARWOOD *is deadly serious.*

MARWOOD: What papers, Danny?

DANNY reaches for his satchel. MARWOOD *grabs it and empties it out on the table. The usual flotsam of food and make up. Also the National Assistance envelopes and a legal-looking document.*

He's got our cheques.

WITHNAIL is too gone to care. The carrot glows like a log.

What are you doing with these?

DANNY: I was gonna cash 'em in for ya.

MARWOOD tries to look reasonably at the document. Juan's shipment gets in the way. And so does

PRESUMING ED. *He starts spinning* WITHNAIL's *globe with both hands. And chanting to himself with a voice as deep as a well,* 'Rama. Rama. Harry Rama . . .'

MARWOOD: For Christ's sake, stop laughing, Withnail. This is a notice of eviction.

PRESUMING ED: Rama. Rama.

WITHNAIL: Give it to my barrister.

PRESUMING ED: Rama. Rama. Harry Rama.

PRESUMING ED's *religious ceremony increases the fury of* WITHNAIL's *hysterics. And heightens* MARWOOD's *anxiety. He stares at the vast spade spinning Withnail's world around with all the dreadful connotations inherent in it.* MARWOOD *has gone a proverbial whiter shade of pale. The old black magic is throbbing through his veins. A certain breathlessness is evident. Looks like he's in for a dose.*

MARWOOD: Stop laughing. They're throwing us out.

PRESUMING ED: Harry Rama. Harry Rammer. Harry Ramma. Hammy Kalma. Hammy Rammer.

And still the world spins as MARWOOD *tries to maintain sanity.*

MARWOOD: For God's sake, shut up will you. You're giving me the fear.

He charges the window. Opens it. A warlike blast of pneumatics from the construction site. This is worse. He closes it again.

Gimme a downer, Danny. My brain's capsizing. I've gone and fucked my brain.

DANNY: Change down, man. Find your neutral space. You gotta rush. It'll pass. Be seated.

MARWOOD *takes his advice. Stares at* DANNY *with a clenched jaw. The barrister is calmly finishing this*

huge carrot on his own. Teeth are exposed in a smile.
WITHNAIL *makes a slow re-entry.*

MARWOOD: Aren't you getting absurdly high?

DANNY: Precisely the reason I'm smokin' it.

WITHNAIL: Christ, that was funny.

He crawls back to the sofa. Gets offered the carrot. It's refused.

Couldn't. I'm spaced.

DANNY: Not as spaced as your rodents.

MARWOOD: Don't talk about them.

DANNY: I imagine they're talkin' to each other.

MARWOOD: What d'you mean?

DANNY: I dealt with them.

MARWOOD: Dealt with them. What the fuck d'you mean?

DANNY: Dosed 'em. I expect they're dead down the drain.

Electricity increases voltage. MARWOOD *is losing control again.*

MARWOOD: *Dead down the drain.* What have you done to them?

DANNY: Given 'em all drugged onions.

MARWOOD: *Jesus Christ.* Why have you drugged their onions?

DANNY: Sit down, man. Take control.

MARWOOD: Gimme a Valium. I'm getting the fear.

DANNY: You have done something to your brain. You have made it high. If I lay ten mills of Diazepam on you, you will do something else to your brain. You will make it low. Why trust one drug and not the other?

Reality floods on WITHNAIL. *He reaches for the legal document.*

That's politics, isn't it?

123

MARWOOD: I'm gonna eat some sugar.

And he beetles off into the kitchen with DANNY *speaking after him.*

DANNY: I recommend you smoke some more grass.

MARWOOD (*O.S.*): No way. No fucking way.

DANNY: That is an unfortunate political decision, reflecting these times.

WITHNAIL: What are you talking about, Danny?

DANNY: Politics, man. If you're hanging on to a rising balloon, you're presented with a difficult decision.

The joint has gone out and he relights it and takes a big hit.

Let go before it's too late? Or hang on and keep getting higher? Posing the question, how long can you keep a grip on the rope?

MARWOOD *returns spooning sugar from a bag. But he doesn't rejoin the group.* WITHNAIL *is no longer smiling. But going down.*

They're selling hippy wigs in Woolworth's, man. The greatest decade in the history of mankind is over.

Another lung-shattering hit and he passes the joint to PRESUMING.

And as Presuming Ed here has so consistently pointed out, we have failed to paint it black.

108. INT. BEDROOM. APARTMENT. DAY.

Big close up of an old suitcase on the bed. It's already almost full and hands stuff the last few items in. The last sock. The last crumpled shirt. The battered notebook. Written on the cover in black ink is 'Withnail and I'. The lid of the ancient case is closed and the catches snapped shut. *A hand reaches for a black trilby on the bed post. The hat journeys across the room and* MARWOOD's *face is finally revealed. He stares at himself in a mirror. His head sports a 1914 cut – hard to get used to after such a mane. One thing he doesn't look is happy. He turns away. Rain is drumming on the window. What few possessions he has are packed in cardboard boxes. He picks up his case and pauses at the door. A last look around the room he knows he'll never see again.*

109. INT. LIVING ROOM. APARTMENT. DAY.
WITHNAIL *looks up from the sofa as* MARWOOD *walks in. Nothing said because there isn't much to say. But the eyes are saying a lot. Both are aware this is it. It is time to say goodbye.*

MARWOOD: My dad'll pick up the boxes in the week, and he's gonna do something about the car.

WITHNAIL *nods and smiles a bit. And* MARWOOD *smiles a bit back.*

Well, I'm off now, then.

WITHNAIL: Already?

And he suddenly animates and is gonna make it harder than it is.

I've got us a bottle open.

He flourishes it with great glee. MARWOOD *clearly wants to leave.*

I confiscated it from Monty's supplies. Fifty-three Margaux, best of the century. I'm sure he wouldn't resent us a parting drink.

He's about to fill a pair of waiting glasses. But MARWOOD *doesn't want to wait. Wants the goodbye over with and wants out of here.*

MARWOOD: I can't, Withnail. I've gotta walk to the station. I'll be late.

WITHNAIL: There's always time for a glass.

MARWOOD: No. I don't have the time.

WITHNAIL: All right. I'll walk you through the park, we can drink it on the way.

The last thing MARWOOD *wanted to hear. But* WITHNAIL *is already climbing into his overcoat and scarf and grabs his brolly to leave.*

110. EXT. REGENT'S PARK. CAMDEN TOWN. DAY.
The park is as bleak and deserted as it's ever been. The afternoon is dissolving into threadbare rain. They walk the paths like they've done a dozen times before. But they were together then. And now they're already alone. Strangers already. And the sweet and sour music is but an addition to the wider sentiment.

MARWOOD *carries his battered suitcase.* WITHNAIL *his battered black umbrella. His bottle is half drunk and he attempts to hand it over again. But this time* MARWOOD *shakes his head.*

MARWOOD: No. No more, thanks.

So WITHNAIL *drinks another mouthful.* MARWOOD *is almost in pain.*

Listen, Withnail. It's a stinker. Why don't you go back?

WITHNAIL: Because I wanna walk you to the station.

MARWOOD: Well, don't. Please, don't.

They stop and stare at each other. Just the sound of rain beating on the umbrella . . .

I really don't want you to.

The vacuum has been burst and there's a lot of silence

about. MARWOOD *lays a hand on his friend's shoulder. Almost a whisper.*
I shall miss you, Withnail.
And the sadness has finally hit and WITHNAIL *is looking bleak.*
WITHNAIL: I shall miss you too. Chin-chin.
He offers a toast and drinks and MARWOOD *turns and walks away.* WITHNAIL *watches him evaporate into rain. He doesn't look back.*

Just the sound of rain beating on the umbrella.
WITHNAIL *walks a little way with his bottle and almost inadvertently finds himself in front of the wolves' cage. He hangs wrists over the railings staring at the pissed-off wolves. They stare back looking as sad as him. He addresses one with a profound lack of sentiment.*
I have of late, but wherefore I know not, lost all my mirth.
And the fifty-three again journeys to his lips. The wolf keeps staring. WITHNAIL *keeps speaking like a natural instinct.*
And indeed, it goes so heavily with my disposition, that this goodly frame the earth, seems to me a sterile promontory.
Now the wine is adding some volume. This is WITHNAIL *back in gear. And all his pride and rage is adding emotion.*
This most excellent canopy the air, look you, this brave o'erhanging firmament, this majestical roof fretted with golden fire, why it appeareth nothing to me but a foul and pestilent congregation of vapours.
WITHNAIL *is suddenly on a stage somewhere. Obviously at Stratford. And his expression asks: And by God, I'd*

be good enough, wouldn't I? Absolutely brilliant, wouldn't I? No more sadness now. All the fire is back. And all the power!

What a piece of work is a man, how noble in reason, how infinite in faculties, how like an angel in apprehension, how like a god.

He looks at the wolves in wonder that the bastards aren't clapping.

The beauty of the world; the paragon of animals; and yet to me, what is this quintessence of dust? Man delights not me, no, nor women, neither . . . nor women neither.

Albert Finney never felt so good. He takes a last and final slug at the bottle and casts it aside. By Christ, that was the best rendition of Hamlet the world will ever see! The only pity was it was only wolves that saw it. They stare at WITHNAIL *through the bars. He bids them a silent good afternoon and walks away.*

P.O.V. wolves. WITHNAIL *walks across the park until he is a tiny figure in the distance. The sweet and sour music rises into appropriate orchestral perfection as he finally, and far away, disappears.*